DR. KENNETH R. LENZ, CPA, MBA, PHD

Transforming Entrepreneurship

How to build a world-changing business as a Christian

First published by Entrepreneur Leadership Institute 2021

Copyright © 2021 by Dr. Kenneth R. Lenz, CPA, MBA, PhD

All rights reserved. This book or any portion thereof may not be reproduced or used in any manner whatsoever without the express written permission of the author, except for the use of brief quotations in a book review.

Published in Pleasant Garden, North Carolina by Entrepreneur Leadership Institute. Library of Congress Control Number 2021913095

Publisher Note and Legal Disclaimer: All biographical material in this book was obtained from published sources, and as such is not officially approved by the subjects themselves, whether living or deceased. While every attempt was made to ensure the information is accurate, the publisher and author are not responsible for any error or omissions, or for any results obtained from the use of this information.

Scripture quotations are from the ESV® Bible (The Holy Bible, English Standard Version®), copyright © 2001 by Crossway, a publishing ministry of Good News Publishers. Used by permission. All rights reserved.

Library of Congress Cataloging-in-Publication Data is available upon request.

For more information and to purchase books and courses, visit us at www.EntrepreneurLeadership.net

First edition

ISBN: 978-1-7359810-5-5

This book was professionally typeset on Reedsy. Find out more at reedsy.com

Contents

It Starts Here — xi
    Transforming Entrepreneurs — xiii
    My Story — xiii
    What We'll Cover in This Book — xv

I Creativity

1 Opportunity Recognition Part I — 3
    Disruptive Innovation in Different Facets of Business — 3
    Human Resources — 6
    Opportunity Recognition — 8

2 Opportunity Recognition Part II — 12
    Finding Opportunities for Innovation — 12
    Ideate — 17
    Transform — 18
    Schedule — 21

3 Understanding Risk — 23
    Transforming Work and Control — 24
    The Three Stewards and a Chinese Pictogram — 25
    God is a Risk-Taker — 28
    Transforming Failure — 28
    Gambling vs. Risk — 30
    Types of Risk — 31

	Managing Risk Challenges	33
4	Triple Loop Learning & Design Thinking	35
	Triple Loop in Action	37
	Deviations	38
	Examples	39
5	Key Learning Practices	42
	What are the eight key learning practices each entrepreneur should encourage among employees and perhaps your vendors?	42
6	Protecting Your Ideas	48
	Non-Disclosure Agreements	48
	Non-Compete Agreement	49
	Monopoly Rights	50
	Royalties and Licensing	52

II Marketing

7	Testing Viability	55
	Testing the Market	55
	Applying Survey Results in Action	57
	Test Ads	58
	Responding to Customer Feedback	59
	Solving Customer Needs	60
	Customer Expectations	62
	Competitors	62
	Nonprofit Organizations	62
8	Advertising & Social Media	65
	Sell the Sizzle	65
	An Example	66
	Other Forms of Advertisement	67

	Marketing as Christian	69
9	Sales	72
	Gathering Customer Information	72
	Transforming Price Setting	74
	Sales Force Staffing	76
	Nonprofit Organizations	77
	Sales Cycle Pipeline	77
	Marketplace Awareness	79
	Delays Closing the Sale	79
	Sale	82
	Unrealistic Expectations	82
	Work in Process (WIP)	83
	Write-Downs	84
	Accounts Receivable	84
	Cash	85
	Priming the Pump	86
10	Strategies & Distribution Channels	87
	Wholesale Distribution	87
	Retail Customers	88
	Websites and Network Sales	89
	Franchise Models	89
	Licensing	90
	Integrated Channel	91
	Choosing Your Distribution Channels	91
	Creating Sales Synergy	93
	Selecting Your Strategy	93
	Pipeline Metrics	94
	The Bigger Picture	99

III Operations

11	Systems Thinking	105
	Cycles	105
	Illustration	107
	Efficiency Improvements	108
	Illustration	112
	Measuring	113
	Final Thoughts	114
12	Lean Operations	116
	Effectiveness and Efficiency	116
	Lean Operations	117
	Just In Time	118
	Kanban	119
	Kaizen	120
	The Hedgehog Concept	120
	Triple Loop Learning Theory	121
	Queuing Theory	122
13	Supply Chain Management	127
	Blended Employee and Vendor Startups	129
	Partnering	132
	Logistics	133
14	Automation & Outsourcing	135
	Customer Interaction	135
	Designing Your Business Operations	139

IV Accounting & Finances

15	The 3 Key Financial Statements: The Balance Sheet	147
	Introduction to the Balance Sheet	149

	Insights of the Balance Sheet	153
16	The 3 Key Financial Statements: Profit & Loss Statement	157
17	The 3 Key Financial Statements: Cash Flow Statement	167
18	Choosing Your Method	174
19	Dashboards & Ratios	182
	Current Ratio	183
	Quick Ratio	183
	Inventory Turnover Ratio	184
	ROI	184
	Debt to Equity Ratio	185
	Times Interest Earned Ratio	185
	Accounts Receivable Turnover Ratio	186
	Dashboards	187
20	Choosing Your Business Entity	190
	Sole Proprietorship	191
	Partnership	191
	Corporations	193
	Limited Liability Company	195
	Business Trust	196
	The Liechtenstein Trust	197
	Specific Problem Areas for Your Business Entity	198
	What Kind of Business Entity Should You Choose?	199
	An Example	201
21	Taxes and Regulations	202
	What kind of taxes should you expect?	203
	Payroll Taxes	206
	VAT and Sales Taxes	207

	Use Tax	208
	Personal Property Tax	209
	Customs Reports and Duties	209
	Transfer Pricing	209
	Tax Audits and Tax Collection	210
	Information Returns	211
	Missed tax payments	212
	Trust Fund Taxes	212
	Labor Law and Safety Law Requirements	213
	Optional Filings	215
22	Financing Options	217
	Creative Financing	218
	Lending Companies	219
	Financing Stages	220
	Government Programs	221
	Selling Stock	224
	Unique Challenges of Nonprofits and Charitable Organizations	228

V	Cross-Cultural Leadership	
23	Building Corporate Culture & Goal Setting	233
	National Culture	233
	Organizational Culture	237
	Motivation	239
	Setting Goals	242
24	Employee Development	247
	Offering Benefits and Incentives	250
	Spiritual Support and Outreach	253
	Nonprofits	256

25	Vendor Development	258
	Keiretsu	259
	Partnering	259
	Integrating Vendors	260
26	Peer Accountability & Community Involvement	263
	Accountability	264
	Community	266

VI   Business Modeling

27	Unique Value Proposition	271
	Value Proposition	271
	Customer	272
	People	273
	Technology	273
	Unique Advantages	274
	Revising Your Plans	277
	An Example	278
28	Core Competency Design	281
	Laying the Foundation	282
	An Example	285
29	"Failure" and Refining	290
	Rethinking Your Ideas	291
	How to Pivot	294
	Why Startups Fail — Or Succeed	296
30	Uses for Plans & Budgets	299
	Executive Summary	301
	Mission	302
	Core Values	302
	Goals & Objectives	303
	Industry Description & Analysis	304

	Market Analysis	305
	Marketing & Sales Plan	306
	Management Team	306
	Operations Plan	307
	Financial Projections	307
	Non-Financial Measurement Criteria	309
	Risk Factors	310
	Exit Strategy	311
31	Risk, Finance, & Christian Values	312
	Measuring Progress with Non-Financial Goals	313
	Rockefeller Foundation	314
	Business entities	314
	Qualitative Measurements	315
	Quantitative Systems	316
	Social Return On Investment (SROI)	317
	What Really Matters	324
32	Spiritual Goal Setting	325
	Transforming Goal Setting with the Great Commission	326
	Matthew 28:18-20	327
	Deuteronomy 6:8-9	328
	James 1:22-25	329
	Operational Cycles	331
	Case Study	332

What's Next	335
Continue Learning	336
About the Author	338

It Starts Here

If you are reading this book, you are most likely already a Christian entrepreneur or are considering becoming one. You have the potential—or perhaps you have already begun—to transform people's lives and hearts by living out the Gospel in a way that creates jobs, spurs progress, provides needed goods and services, and most importantly points others to Christ.

Becoming an entrepreneur is exciting and strenuous, but ultimately very rewarding, both during the journey itself and when you have achieved your definition of success. The path of entrepreneurship is extremely flexible with many possible routes and various definitions of success. Yet there are some basic concepts which all entrepreneurs must consider that are rarely explained clearly to future business owners. This is one of the reasons I am writing this book—to provide you with a guide for increasing your probability of success in launching and leading your own company or organization.

As a Christian entrepreneur, I have a second goal for writing this book. I hope to help you see how entrepreneurship can be a platform for marketplace ministry. It is a platform to reach many people who might not otherwise hear and experience the saving Gospel message of Jesus. To be effective evangelists in the marketplace, following in the footsteps of powerful examples like the Apostle Paul, we must intentionally integrate discipleship practices holistically into all aspects of our businesses.

Finding a good book that provides both the theory and the practical "street-level" insight into building a successful company is hard. Finding a book like that in the form of a practical guide from the perspective of a seasoned Christian entrepreneur is even harder.

That's why I created Entrepreneur Leadership Institute. And that's why I wrote this book. I want to provide a practical guidebook for integrating your faith as a Christian leader in the business world, through entrepreneurship. I want to teach you the theory, show you the practical steps, and guide you in the Biblical principles that will help you transform your business, your community, and the world.

This book provides a framework assisting you in methodically developing either a business or charitable organization that can achieve both goals—providing temporal improvements for you and your community while generating eternal benefits for individuals whom you have the opportunity to influence through your business connections. If you are saved, God is at work transforming your life. He has called you to participate in that work and in the work of transforming the world. Are you ready to transform the way you do business?

Let's begin!

Transforming Entrepreneurs

"Do not be conformed to this world, but be transformed by the renewal of your mind, that by testing you may discern what is the will of God, what is good and acceptable and perfect." — Romans 12:2

In my book *Transforming Entrepreneurs*, we learned from the stories of Christian entrepreneurs who transformed society. We walked with them as they overcame challenges: racism, sexism, poverty, illness, tragedy, and more. They were transformed by the Gospel and through that, despite all odds, they transformed the world. The world we live in today is their legacy.

And the same God who was at work in their lives is at work in ours. He offers total transformation to each and every one of us. And when we let Him transform our hearts and lives, he equips us — by the truth of His Word and the power of His Holy Spirit in us — to transform the world around us.

In this book, I'm distilling my years of entrepreneurial experience and training as a CPA, MBA, and Ph.D. into a guidebook for how to begin—or improve—your business as a Christian.

My Story

Before I lay out what we'll be exploring together in this book, let me introduce myself. My name is Dr. Kenneth Lenz. I've started many companies, non-profit organizations, and am a co-founder of a municipal government. I'm a CPA who has started, led, and sold several accounting and consulting firms across the United States. My firms have focused on providing services to smaller and rapidly growing entrepreneurial firms in various parts of the United States and several other continents. As a capstone to all of this, I earned a Ph.D. in entrepreneurial leadership.

From this unique background, I have studied and been deeply involved with entrepreneurship from the perspective of a serial entrepreneur in a variety of industries—as an adviser to many small business owners, and as a government official writing laws that affected business owners, in the profit-oriented as well as social entrepreneurship (social and governmental) sectors of the economy.

I have taught online business, entrepreneurship, and leadership courses on the bachelors, masters, and doctoral levels for universities in America and Europe. From these many-faceted viewpoints on entrepreneurship, I have also been involved in the international marketplace ministry movement for more than 20 years as a Christian entrepreneur.

Currently, I am the chairman and founder of the Entrepreneur Leadership Institute. This small international research institute conducts innovative research in entrepreneurial leadership and shares those findings with entrepreneurs like you around the world to help you improve society—both temporally and eternally. I am currently developing a division of the Entrepreneur Leadership Institute which will offer training for Christians who desire to start and grow new businesses that can also engage in sharing the Gospel in the marketplace.

What We'll Cover in This Book

Section 1: Creativity

Why start with creativity when starting a new company or organization? Creativity is a critical portion of self-management. All Christian entrepreneurial enterprises begin with the personal, God-inspired creative thoughts of the founding entrepreneur before any organization is built. The organization blossoms from the mind of the entrepreneur. So this is where we begin.

The chapters within this section explore the key aspects of creative development, which should be an ongoing activity, not a "once and done" type of project. The process of innovation breaks down into four parts:

Part 1 — How can you boost the likelihood of developing an innovative and financially sustainable solution to a challenge? (Chapters 1 and 2)

Part 2 — Risk can have a major impact on sustainability and practical implementation of your idea, but risk can further creativity as well. (Chapter 3)

Part 3 — What methods encourage constant systematic development of new creative thoughts? (Chapter 4 and 5)

Part 4 — Innovative ideas can give your new firm a competitive advantage, but since your brainstorming thoughts can be copied by others, we will review the main methods entrepreneurs utilize to protect their ideas. (Chapter 6)

Section 2: Marketing

"Nothing happens until dollars come in the door." It is easy to spend money, but it is hard to convince customers to voluntarily give you cash.

Marketing looks at how to convey your message about what you are offering and common principles in making and completing actual sales. This crucial section is detailed as follows:

Chapter 7. Testing Viability – Before investing any significant money into infrastructure costs, you should determine how much demand might currently exist for your proposed product or service. There are a couple of exceptions to this general rule, which this chapter will also cover, as well as how to test the public demand.

Chapter 8. Advertising & Social Media – Educating potential customers about your offerings is a form of pre-sales, generating interest among people. This effort is a more complicated, bifurcated educational challenge for charitable organizations than for-profit corporations, although this same dual effort can sometimes apply to Christian businesses.

Chapter 9. Sales – Let's make the deal and collect the

cash! This chapter explores the sales cycle or process, typical time lags, "leakage" in the collections pipeline, and other challenges to this most difficult aspect of launching a new enterprise.

Chapter 10. Strategies & Distribution Channels – It is more effective to focus on specific sources of potential sales to maximize the potential return on marketing and sales-related efforts than to push scattered sales to individual customers.

Section 3: Operations

Operational issues involve how you will provide the products and services offered for sale or provided possibly free as a charity. Since the many different industries, locations, types of operations, and other variables vary so widely, these four chapters approach this section from developing systems-based efforts to efficiently organize your production efforts. Here is a brief overview of each chapter in this section:

Chapter 11. Systems Thinking – Operational efforts need to be as efficient as possible. Part of this effort is to consider each action within your company to be part of a cycle of related activities repeated regularly, or a systematic methodology.

Chapter 12. Lean Operations – Another aspect of operations is efficiency. How can you keep costs as low as possible and processes quick, while maintaining high quality?

Chapter 13. Supply Chain Management – Your vendor sources of materials are critical. This chapter covers the theories most helpful to smaller enterprises for setting up and managing your buyer actions.

Chapter 14. Automation & Outsourcing – Often it is cheaper and from a management perspective less time-consuming to automate some operational processes or allow outside organizations to provide either core or non-core operational efforts. However, we will also discuss the potential downsides of such choices.

Section 4: Accounting and Finances

Accounting is essential for success. It is the language of business. You must track your performance. If you cannot speak the language you cannot understand what you need to focus on. A basic understanding of accounting is required by taxing authorities and can be required by bankers or investors. But you should want to understand your own performance in a timely manner so you can quickly correct errors and take full advantage of new opportunities. We break down the accounting area and your financing options in this section as follows:

Part 1 — The 3 Key Financial Statements – There are three financial statements that tell you and anyone else you must report to how efficient and sustainable your company or charity is. Every entrepreneur should have a basic understanding of bookkeeping to know how the financial statements are developed, other possible financial reports, and the types of messages each of these statements tell you. (chapters 15, 16, 17, 18)

Part 2 — Dashboards & Ratios – Over the past decade, the trend has been to mix traditional accounting data with both non-accounting statistics plus non-traditional accounting and sometimes cost-accounting financial data in a summarized management dashboard. Entrepreneurs can drill down on each statistic to analyze greater detail when needed. (Chapters 19 and 20)

Part 3 — Taxes & Regulation – Governments have made taxation a painful and complicated element of leading both a business and a non-profit organization. Politicians have been very creative in finding new ways to extract taxes from entrepreneurs, so no book can possibly cover every tax in the United States, let alone if you engage in international transactions. However, there are broad categories of taxes and commonly assessed taxes covered in this chapter so you can avoid hefty penalties for accidental non-compliance. (Chapter 21)

Part 4 — Financing Options – At several points during your startup and early growth years, you will need to obtain financing. This chapter explores the various options you might consider for financing either a for-profit or non-profit corporation and their implications. (Chapter 22)

Section 5: Cross-Cultural Leadership

We started this book by pointing out that every entrepreneurial startup begins with the individual entrepreneur's personal leadership. In fact, great organizational leadership is essential. Recognizing that no individuals - not even entrepreneurs - excel at everything, this section covers how you can build leadership skills in other people connected to your company. Entrepreneurs overwhelmingly are self-confident individuals who have no need for peer approval (an intrinsic rather than extrinsic basis of motivation). Still, as Christian leaders, we can benefit from peer accountability, especially in an increasingly cross-cultural workplace and communities. We probe the leadership section by examining the following four areas:

Chapter 23. Building Corporate Culture & Goal Setting – One of the highest reasons entrepreneurs launch their own companies is to reflect their own beliefs and freedom to pursue them. We will examine how you can intentionally create goals and culture to reflect your interests, especially a Bible-influenced workplace that can have a lasting impact in your community.

Chapter 24. Employee Development – Leading employees involves much more than providing orders and structuring financial and fringe benefit incentives. This chapter gives you principles and theories for developing motivated and focused employees. For non-profits, there is an additional element of management and development for volunteer "employees."

Chapter 25. Vendor Enhancement – There is a fuzzy line between employees and vendors in many entrepreneurial organizations. Startup companies need to be very flexible and develop suppliers as partners in growing a business.

Chapter 26. Peer Accountability & Community Involvement – Leadership involves more than giving direction and motivation to others. You should also actively and regularly pursue self-improvement, particularly regarding the Christian aspect of your entrepreneurial endeavors.

Section 6: Business Modeling

Let's put everything we have learned together to create synergy for your efforts. This final section looks at fully progressing from your initial idea into refining and filling out that idea (or some modification of your original thought), to writing a plan that guides you towards achieving your vision.

Part 1 — Unique Value Proposition – As we explored in the first section, you should begin with an innovative idea, but that idea must be proven practical. Now we flesh out the entire idea so we can test whether it is marketable. (Chapter 27)

Part 2 — Core Competency Design – Everything must come together to create success. This chapter reviews methods for connecting marketing, operations, leadership, innovation, and other aspects into a core from which you can expand rapidly. (Chpater 28)

Part 3 — "Failure" and Refining – What is failure? Entrepreneurs realize most people do not understand this concept and its connection to refining your ideas. Very few entrepreneurs succeed with their original concept intact. We will cover how to transition successfully when necessary, as well as some guidelines on when to stubbornly insist on holding the line. (Chapter 29)

Part 4 — Uses for Plans & Budgets – Plans are sometimes required by funding sources. Even when they are not, an initial plan can be useful to help you keep on track towards achieving your vision or at least getting off the launch pad. This final chapter explores both the useful aspects of planning as well as the drawbacks. (Chpaters 30, 31, 32, and 33)

There's a lot of ground to cover. So, let's get to work!

I

Creativity

This section explores the four key aspects of creative development.

Chapters 1 & 2 explore opportunity recognition.

Chapter 3 guides you in understanding risk.

Chapters 4 & 5 explore systematic development.

Chapter 6 teaches you how to protect your ideas.

1

Opportunity Recognition Part I

Disruptive Innovation in Different Facets of Business

Many people mistakenly assume luck is the major factor in big entrepreneurial success. While you cannot control all the circumstances around you, most of the variables are within your control. Let's begin with the "big idea" that might make you rich.

Research demonstrates you are highly unlikely to stumble upon that "big idea," even less likely than winning that billion-dollar lottery from buying one lone ticket. So, in this first chapter, we will explore the theories behind identifying opportunities and then proceed to explain the practical steps you can utilize to generate more opportunities.

The first concept you should understand is called **Disruptive Innovation**. This theory refers to creative ideas which establish new markets, replacing or seriously disrupting existing commercial forums. Do not assume innovation is always a technological advancement. Disruptive innovation can occur in other facets of business, whether marketing, operations, finance, human resources, or other aspects of leading a business organization.

Marketing

For example, John Wannamaker pioneered advertising his store and its products in local Philadelphia newspapers. Today this does not seem like much of a disruptive innovation, but during John's lifetime in the early 1800s, it was. Up to that time, nobody had tried such a radical concept. At first, other business owners mocked him over the apparent huge waste of money. But John demonstrated that his small store could grow rapidly into a regional chain of large department stores through such an innovative idea. As of the writing of this book, this idea has been considered standard business practice in most of the world for almost two centuries.

Operations

Operations is another area where disruptive innovation has substantially changed business behavior. A great example is Sam Walton. His method included:

1. Cutting profit margins far below competing general stores.
2. Making up the difference in both volumes.
3. Carefully designing logistical systems that minimize costs by making volume purchases, creating incentives for store managers to turn over inventory rapidly.
4. Managing truck routes to deliver the product to each store in the shortest amount of time and with the lowest fuel and driver salary costs.

Walton's products are nothing especially distinguishable from competitors' products. His idea was rooted in the operational design of his company, which allowed him to give customers such great bargain prices that most competitors were unable to match his deals. Modern retail stores, often called "big box" stores, have either matched his approach to some extent (Target, Best Buy, etc.), or their lack of innovation has driven them out of business (Toys R Us, Sears, etc.).

Finances

How might finances provide a disruptive innovation that creates a large competitive advantage for the entrepreneur and big savings for customers? Most wholesale and retail companies now apply an idea known as JIT – Just In Time inventory delivery.

No single entrepreneur has taken credit for this disruptive innovation. However, the first hint of this idea arose in Japan, where manufacturing companies hired famed consultant Peter Drucker to improve product quality and manufacturing line efficiency. That led to the Toyota engineers' innovative practice called Kaizen Events – a periodic and systematic approach involving all factory workers to identify and cut wasteful actions.

Eventually, this prompted the question of how manufacturers could reduce or possibly even eliminate all inventory. They quickly answered the question: timing the delivery of raw materials and the shipping of sold finished goods, so the product moved swiftly through the manufacturing plant, leaving little held on shelves and factory floors. An accountant eventually asked the next logical Kaizen question about payment and collection policies.

Within a few years, American companies implemented the new JIT approach beyond the factory floor: Every day, they paid for raw materials shortly after delivery at the moment factory workers were ready to use those materials. Simultaneously, they offered discounts to customers who paid promptly or with an advanced deposit.

The formerly large amounts of capital tied up in inventory on corporate balance sheets are now released, saving interest expense on credit lines no longer fully utilized. For some companies with high gross profit margins, the JIT applications to finance provided enough customer advances to cover the cost of paying for raw materials later.

Companies could increase their competitive advantage by reducing product sales prices while also using the newly freed cash to either grow the business much faster or provide shareholders with more generous dividends. Again, this innovation, while disrupting the financing and banking industries, is now considered a standard "best practices" idea that all finance departments should implement.

Human Resources

Ross Perot provides us with a great example of disruptive innovation in the human resources aspect of business. In the 1980s, this failed IBM salesman lost his job because IBM was losing most of its remuneration. Most companies at that time were already transitioning away from huge and vastly expensive mainframe computers into the much smaller and more affordable mini and microcomputers.

To capitalize on the opportunity of companies getting rid of their expensive mainframe computers, Ross successfully talked several former customers into selling their mainframe computers to him. And he sweetened the deal—convincing them to outsource IT operations. Now, entire IT departments (which would previously have been in-house at a corporation) were outsourced to Ross. The corporation benefited from the services Ross provided, and saved money by not having to employ an entire department.

Each company operation by itself was a big money loser. But Ross laid off some personnel, sold some computers for losses, and sold the excess capacity on the remaining large frame computers to provide services, particularly accounting and payroll services that all companies operated in the same manner.

This disruptive idea cost IBM sales, and some employees from other companies had to find new jobs, but Ross created the outsourcing industry, and his company, Automated Data Processing (ADP). It is now a multi-billion dollar company employing many thousands of people in well-paid jobs, helping communities to prosper while saving client companies significant amounts of overhead expenses.

Opportunity Recognition

All of these examples illustrate how entrepreneurs have recognized opportunities and responded by transforming businesses and industries with disruptive innovations. There were both negative and positive outcomes of these innovations. Some criticize the negative effects while others say the positive benefits outweigh any downsides. In the next chapter, we will explore this debate.

Disruptive Innovations: Positive or Negative?

Hopefully, you can see how the concept of Disruptive Innovation can apply to any and every area of a business. I would like to provide one more example to illustrate the potential of both the positive and negative aspects of Disruptive Innovation.

Henry Ford did not invent the automobile, contrary to popular myth. In fact, several other people and companies in both Europe and America had started producing "horseless carriages," as automobiles were then called, approximately a decade before Henry decided to enter this industry. So why is Henry credited with inventing the automobile?

For the previous decade, only the wealthy could afford a custom-built car. Henry's disruptive idea was to lay out an assembly line across the building where his workers would do the same repetitive tasks all day long every day. This streamlined innovation. Rather than moving between tasks like a traditional craftsman would when creating a product, each individual would be assigned a specific part of the labor and stick to it, to help build the entire car.

Today this mass production assembly line sounds like common sense, but at that time Henry's idea was truly disruptive and not well accepted in some areas of the economy. Henry could standardize the cars he produced and achieved a high volume of product, thus he cut the cost well below what existing custom car manufacturers could compete with. He also paid five dollars a day to each of his factory workers – a rate well above what other employers were willing or able to pay.

Henry intended to create a mass market for his product quickly. While he initially lost the high-margin niche of custom automobiles for wealthy people, his hunch proved wildly successful. Now average workers, including his own factory workers, could afford his lower-priced cars.

He had two key strengths: 1) a lower profit margin, and 2) an expanded market for the product. Effectively, one created the other. A lower profit margin made for lower prices, and opened up a market size more than a hundred times what the automobile market had been previously, when it catered to rich individuals who could afford the luxury of an automobile. Yet, it still created vast wealth for Henry personally, while single-handedly raising the standard of living for the overwhelming majority of Americans. To put this in perspective, his workers earned approximately $800 monthly, or twice the amount he sold his assembly line cars for.

What about those who were hurt by Henry's disruptive innovation idea? Certainly, he put many buggy whips and carriage manufacturers out of business. He drastically reduced the demand for horse-related products and services, drove many town stables out of business, and created unemployment among farriers and coachmen. Economists estimate Henry's idea cost job losses of around 400,000.

But in the process of eliminating those 400,000 jobs, Henry personally generated over 1,000,000 jobs and created entirely new higher-paying professions such as automotive engineers and efficiency experts. In addition, his idea created an impressive number of industries, such as gas stations, convenience stores, auto repair shops, and others. Small existing industries suddenly expanded on a massive scale, such as gasoline production (including oil exploration, well drilling, drilling rig manufacturing, pipeline and refining companies such as Rockefeller's Standard Oil Company, and related oil industries).

The mass-produced passenger car led to mass-produced vehicles to transport goods more directly and cheaply: Trucks. That in turn cut costs of goods, due to lower transport costs while making formerly luxury goods available to nearly everyone on-demand and at more easily affordable prices—even in the most remote parts of the nation.

City transportation also became quicker, more affordable, and customized with the rise of the taxicab industry, thanks to Henry. Faster and cheaper transport costs significantly improved the reach of traveling salesmen offering a much greater variety of products at ever more affordable prices, generating greater prosperity throughout the country and abroad.

By the time he died, economists estimated Henry Ford's disruptive idea that cost 400,000 former jobs had also created 8,000,000 new, higher-paying replacement jobs. Most of those 400,000 displaced workers quickly found better jobs in the new economy, thanks to the ripple effect of Henry's disruptive idea. This is not to downplay some personal stories of discomfort which always accompany any new innovation—hence the word "disruptive." But consumers, most workers, and society as a whole were noticeably far better off from Henry's innovative assembly line idea, and the time period for society to adjust to this new paradigm was relatively short.

A compassionate, Christian entrepreneur might have taken an additional step beyond what Henry Ford did. Some of Henry's Christian entrepreneurial contemporaries made the extra effort to use their newly generated wealth towards providing social and spiritual support services to help workers and their families who were temporarily displaced by disruptive innovations to make a quick transition and minimize their discomfort. Some Christian entrepreneurs even provided opportunities for displaced workers to benefit personally from new business opportunities arising as a result of these disruptive innovations.

How do you find opportunities for disruptive innovations like these? We'll discuss this next in part two.

2

Opportunity Recognition Part II

Finding Opportunities for Innovation

We'll now turn to another important concept for understanding how you can find new opportunities. Mathematicians have developed a specialized field of study in dynamic systems under the rubric of **Chaos Theory**. These researchers found that actions that superficially seem to be random can, upon much closer examination, be reduced to a number of extensive logical interactions.

The volume of such interactions makes an observable behavior complex, in spite of the otherwise deterministic functions. Thus the behavior seems random or chaotic. Once you understand that the supposed randomness is nothing more than many complex systems, you begin to recognize that such behaviors can be at least semi-managed towards a more likely optimal result.

To put this in more straightforward terms, try to solve for as many variables as you need to accomplish your goals. You do not need to solve all of them in the matrix, just enough to improve the likelihood of finding an innovative solution that generates a sustainable competitive advantage. While this sounds complex (and it is!) it can be relatively simple in practice. When combined, the Disruptive Innovation concept and an understanding of Chaos Theory provide an insight into where innovative ideas might be uncovered.

But before we move on to the practical steps for improving opportunity recognition, we should cover a few more concepts.

Opportunity can be defined as a set of circumstances making it possible to accomplish something. It can also be characterized as a favorable juncture of circumstances. How you observe a situation and the component variables within that situation allows you to either recognize or miss an opportunity.

For example, many 1800s dairy farmers in the area encompassing western Pennsylvania, northern Ohio, and western New York state complained about water polluted with oil because it made their cows sick and cost them money. John D. Rockefeller observed the same situation, but he saw profit rather than losses from the pollution. Contracting with a professor in Michigan, John found a way to refine that pollution into multiple usable and highly profitable products.

He purchased large amounts of that oil pollution from farmers and refined it into kerosene, and eventually added gasoline, refined oil products, and an entire line of energy-related products that revolutionized transportation, lighting, and many other industries. Even John missed a big opportunity. His crews would allow the deadly, gaseous pollution to escape when they drilled new wells. Eventually, another entrepreneur decided to capture it instead, creating the multi-billion dollar natural gas industry.

Another important concept is **sustainability**. We can define sustainability as the ability to perpetuate or grow something without being completely used up or as a process, service, or product that can be continuously provided and sold, which will last or continue indefinitely.

Obviously, this requires a variety of business components to work together effectively, such as generating sufficient marketing and sales leads to produce enough cash to cover operational costs while producing the goods or services efficiently, and generating enough profit to allow for continued growth and to overcome the unexpected expenditures that inevitably arise in every type of operation.

There are several principles to consider that will help you avoid missing opportunities. As Peter Drucker, the famous management consultant, and researcher, noted, it is more dangerous to ask the wrong question than to get the wrong answer. Thus the need to explore all the variables and consider alternative ways in which a situation might be improved.

In doing so, we should endeavor to avoid two prominent mistakes regarding opportunity recognition: The first is to assume you only need to be creative occasionally. Thomas

Edison, the great inventor and creator of the first "innovation factory or laboratory," highlighted this principle. Many people have heard his comment that he did not fail many times while inventing the light bulb; he first found 10,000 ways it could not be produced.

Fewer people have read that he employed several thousand people in his "invention factory." His employees created other products. Though he directed the experiments, he relied upon employees to conduct the experiments and question the paradigms they were helping Tom explore, such as motion pictures (movies) and the phonograph.

It was Tom's constant push for new innovations and the idea of a laboratory perceived as a type of factory to produce a frequent stream of innovations, whether small or major, that helped him find the major, society-changing, new products as a result of small incremental series of progressions. When you can safely do so without the risk of others stealing your ideas, it is always more effective to ask other people's insights on your ideas, as Tom did.

This points to another important mistake to avoid. Many people hope to find one great idea that will create a massive wealth-generating company. Yet innovation rarely arrives in this manner. For example, Google (now Alphabet) was started by two college students in a dorm room. The search engine giant is approaching a trillion-dollar market valuation today, but the initially struggling dorm-based company nearly went bankrupt, or more accurately insolvent, because of the huge cash burn in its early years.

Those students initially thought they could provide some sort of index or information service that people could search. However, the computing power needs grew rapidly, and there was no obvious source of revenue they could tap to cover the mounting costs of maintaining an increasing number of computers and connections. It took a multitude of smaller "trial and error" adjustments over several years to arrive at today's powerful high-profit search engine service. The founders readily admit they could not have foreseen today's model for quite some time, especially without trying various smaller adjustments in their business model.

When attempting to develop a creative solution to any challenge observed, there are two possible approaches—**problem solving** and **problem finding**.

1. **Problem solving** involves formulating a visual representation of the problem quickly rather than investing most of your time considering various possible solutions to overcome that problem.
2. **Problem finding** takes the reverse approach, investing the bulk of your time exploring questions and issues at length from every viewpoint you and trustworthy others can think of, including a number of unlikely reasons for a situation. Then sketch possible solutions to each of the different angles you thought of.

The most successful innovators report that the problem-finding approach yields the fastest and most effective results over the long term, stimulating more creative ideas since you are not immediately narrowing possibilities to one line of possible causes as the first approach does.

We can group creative idea generation into three areas: **Ideate**, **Transform**, and **Schedule**.

Ideate

Ideate is the effort to think about a problem or challenge comprehensively from differing possible causes or various conceivable ways the situation might react with each other. How many reasons can you dream up for why the situation is the way it seems to be currently? Then consider as many avenues as come to mind for trying to topple each of those situations.

At this early stage of innovation, we are not concerned with how practical or likely your framings of the problem or each of your potential solutions might be. We want to generate as many possibilities – including the highly unlikely ones – as we possibly can.

There are many instances throughout history where the seemingly least likely explanation provided a creative insight—leading to an innovative solution that other people repeatedly overlooked. By considering ways to unseat your explanations of how the variables in the current situation might be interacting, you are not trying to eliminate possible viewpoints but instead hoping to generate more possibilities for why the situation is what it currently seems to be.

Transform

After generating a sufficiently long list of possible explanations describing the current problem, it is time to move on to the next stage—transformation. **Transforming** involves three actions.

We can call the first action **scamper**. Scampering involves brainstorming about all the possible variables involved in the situation. For example, a mid-sized agribusiness client of mine owns hundreds of tractor-trailers. The business involves leaving these trailers at harvesting sites until all crops have been gathered and packaged. Likewise, many trailers are left on a consignment basis with a wide variety of customers (both wholesale and retail) across many locations in a couple of dozen states. How to keep track of this inventory of trailers?

The problem grew out of proportion until it had to be addressed, as the cost of keeping track of all trailers had been prohibitive. However, the company and its related corporations' growth generated the need to find this inventory—a task that seemed onerous. They would need to locate and confirm all the trailers still owned by the company. How could current employees and management do this while continuing to service the rapidly increasing volume of sales and production?

Considering just one possible definition or viewpoint of this problem – how to tag and track trailers in the future as they rotate through a regional warehouse. We could begin to identify possible variables as we "scamper" to understand aspects of this one scenario.

Variables might include:

- A paper tracking system.
- Painting a trailer number on the side of each trailer.
- Using a coding system that limits dispatch of each trailer to a designated state, region, type of customer, etc. for quicker identification.
- A matching of trailer serial numbers to legal titles from the Division of Motor Vehicles.
- Comparison to computerized monthly reports from state transportation weigh scales compared to company and contractor trucking firms' trucks hauling each trailer.
- Customer billing invoices which could add trailer numbers or location.
- Old insurance reports listing trailers covered on policies and trailers reported in accidents or claims.

These are some examples to get you started. Other variables whether major, insignificant, unlikely, and so forth could be explored.

The second action in transforming is to list the attributes for each variable. Considering the same trucking example, look at the first variable we thought of – a paper tracking system. What are all the possible attributes of that variable?

We might want to develop a paper form that includes:

- The truck number and/or driver number
- Trailer number
- Location
- Customer number
- Date sent from warehouse
- Date returned
- Employee signatures to assign responsibility for each other attribute such as who assigned a particular trailer to a unique driver and route
- A trucker signature confirming delivery and pickup of the trailer (or reporting theft or damage of product or the trailer itself)
- Accounting clerk matching customer invoicing to product sent / returned, etc...

Finally, the third action in transforming is to write down all the possible reverses of what you just developed, especially the assumptions. Utilizing this same trucking example, ask yourself:

- Are we asking too many people to sign off on the trailer's progress?
- Do any of these attributes or their variables allow us to account for forgotten trailers that do not make it back to one of the warehouses for long periods of time (or ever)?
- How do we account for a trailer which left one location but was returned to another or quickly reloaded and sent out the same day without our paper tracking system keeping up with the trailer's new assignment?

- Is there a better way to develop a full accounting for all trailers as well as move product (and trailers) faster without losing individual responsibility for each load?

Reversing our initial assumptions may uncover new avenues for solving this problem or might lead us to reject this entire set of variables in favor of a better approach to solving the problem.

As you can see from this simple trucking example, the ideate and transform steps can involve many possible views of the problem and components involved in each view. For example, we have yet to consider GPS electronic tagging or paying someone on a contract basis to visit old and new customer sites, scour police and insurance reports, and perhaps drive around areas where the company has a concentration of customer drop shipping points to develop a list of trailers that may or may not rotate through company warehouses. Providing iPads to truckers is another alternative. When we develop as exhaustive a list as we can initially conceive, we finally advance to the final step—scheduling.

Schedule

Scheduling involves two key things: One, it involves estimating how long it might take to solve the problem, following each of the more likely approaches you have developed in the prior steps. Two, it involves estimating a quota or limit on how many resources you can afford to devote towards solving this problem.

Returning to the trucking example, the company is growing rapidly, and it is primarily an agribusiness company, not a trucking company, although it has several trucking subsidiaries to move its own products. Even if the company can afford to commit a significant amount of money to solve the problem (though this might take away from growth opportunities), the limited employee time assigned to each approach might be a far more restrictive challenge.

Once you have completed all three steps – ideate, transform, and schedule – take a brief break from your brainstorming efforts. In the interim, you could ask other people to review your ideas and comment on them. Reviewing them yourself later with a fresh perspective can also give you more insights. Do not be surprised if you feel the need to reject all the scenarios you developed in this, or possibly a subsequent, round. Developing innovative solutions is mostly hard grunt work rather than "ah-ha!" moments of brilliance.

3

Understanding Risk

Risk and reward are intertwined. The concept of risk is frequently misunderstood by most people, and the concept of reward is often inaccurately defined. However, we will discuss this towards the end of the book. Right now, let's concentrate on the word risk.

Most people consider "risk" to be the possibility of failure, loss, or delay. This is not how entrepreneurs understand the concept of risk. Closely related, entrepreneurs also recognize the idea of failure as something quite different from how most people prefer to define it.

Transforming Work and Control

To begin perceiving these ideas of risk and failure correctly, let us start by exploring underlying concepts which can affect risk and failure. In the early portion of Genesis, God commands Adam and Eve to work – naming animals, accepting stewardship over creation, tilling the ground, becoming fruitful and multiplying, and related tasks. Note that this work assignment predates the fall and may even be expected in heaven where we are told that angels serve God and where there will be a new earth as well as a new heaven.

So it is a good and natural human activity to work, not a consequence of sin. *Work by its nature causes transformation*—hopefully improvement—of the environment around us and should lead to greater productivity and benefits for ourselves and others. This effort is not guaranteed to produce positive results, at least since Adam and Eve first sinned. Perhaps trial and error might have been part of their learning experience prior to departure from the Garden of Eden. Some Christian entrepreneurs have defined work as a God-commanded gift or activity for serving others and improving lives. Again, *transformation.*

Another concept to consider is the locus of **control**. This term refers to one's belief of the extent to which an individual may control or influence the outcome of events around you. Researchers have found that almost nobody believes they can control 100% of what happens around you or to you.

However, if you believe you can have a major influence on

the events in your life and those events are controllable factors such as personal attitude, preparation, and effort expended, you have an internal locus of control, according to the Encyclopedia of Psychology. If you feel your life is mostly out of your personal control and you can only react to the actions and events of others around you, you are said to have an external locus of control. Entrepreneurs have a strong internal locus of control, as do other types of leaders. **As entrepreneurs, we believe that we have the ability to transform our lives, our businesses, and our world.**

The Three Stewards and a Chinese Pictogram

Read the parable of the three stewards found in Matthew 25:14-30.

> "For it will be like a man going on a journey, who called his servants and entrusted to them his property. To one he gave five talents, to another two, to another one, to each according to his ability. Then he went away. He who had received the five talents went at once and traded with them, and he made five talents more. So also he who had the two talents made two talents more. But he who had received the one talent went and dug in the ground and hid his master's money. Now after a long time the master of those servants came and settled accounts with them. And he who had received the five talents came forward, bringing five talents more, saying, 'Master,

you delivered to me five talents; here, I have made five talents more.' His master said to him, 'Well done, good and faithful servant. You have been faithful over a little; I will set you over much. Enter into the joy of your master.' And he also who had the two talents came forward, saying, 'Master, you delivered to me two talents; here, I have made two talents more.' His master said to him, 'Well done, good and faithful servant. You have been faithful over a little; I will set you over much. Enter into the joy of your master.' He also who had received the one talent came forward, saying, 'Master, I knew you to be a hard man, reaping where you did not sow, and gathering where you scattered no seed, so I was afraid, and I went and hid your talent in the ground. Here, you have what is yours.' But his master answered him, 'You wicked and slothful servant! You knew that I reap where I have not sown and gather where I scattered no seed? Then you ought to have invested my money with the bankers, and at my coming I should have received what was my own with interest. So take the talent from him and give it to him who has the ten talents. For to everyone who has will more be given, and he will have an abundance. But from the one who has not, even what he has will be taken away. And cast the worthless servant into the outer darkness. In that place there will be weeping and gnashing of teeth.'

The master took a risk by entrusting his servants with varying amounts of money. The sin described in the parable is not the different amounts of productivity, for we each start with a unique set of talents, family situations, cultural or societal limitations, and other variables. The third servant's sin was his laziness, his failure even to try a bit of work. That final servant's attitude was an external locus of control. He stated his fear of losing the money and unwillingness to undertake any risk. In summary, the third servant had a preservation viewpoint rather than an opportunity-minded one, even though he knew his master expected a return on his investment in the servant.

This parable highlights an essential viewpoint for entrepreneurs. *Business owners are opportunity-focused, not risk-focused.* Therefore they attempt to minimize risk without eliminating it since the risk is a necessary ingredient for innovation. Most people tend to take the opposite viewpoint.

Another way of understanding this view is the Chinese pictogram ☒☒. This traditional pictogram (pronounced "ce-quay" and transliterated into English as "weijl") has the dual meaning of both opportunity and danger, plus it signifies a critical moment. Opportunity and danger or risk are inextricably intertwined into a moment in time that can change the future.

God is a Risk-Taker

Christian entrepreneurs know they can focus on the potential advances while hedging against much of the risk because God Himself provides examples in His character. God is a risk-taker—repeatedly reaching out to flawed humans throughout history to proclaim His Word. The act of creation itself, including giving humans free will, was a huge risk. Risk is the catalyst for transformation.

In all of this, God is also a personal, logical, and careful risk-taker. That shows other characteristics Christian entrepreneurs can emulate – risk analysis is possible to minimize the possibility of not achieving the goal and increasing the probability of success.

Transforming Failure

Before delving into the components of risk, it is important to clearly delineate what "failure" might be. Many people assume failure is losing money, possessions, or being forced into declaring a moral, a financial, or another type of public embarrassment. **Entrepreneurs recognize only one correct definition of the word failure – giving up on your efforts.**

Perhaps somewhat surprising to non-entrepreneurs, most self-made wealthy tycoons have first filed for bankruptcy, lost assets to a repossession, closed a business, or experienced some other form of what other people consider "failure" before achieving great wealth. As Thomas Edison stated, he never "failed" but simply found 10,000 ways the light bulb could not be produced on his way towards uncovering the method that would succeed. Wealth alone is simply not the sole metric an entrepreneur uses to define success.

Perhaps the best illustration of this attitude was President Theodore Roosevelt's famous Sorbonne speech in Paris, France, on April 23, 1910. He proclaimed the passage called "The Man in the Arena," which goes as follows:

> *It is not the critic who counts; not the man who points out how the strong man stumbles, or where the doer of deeds could have done them better. The credit belongs to the man who is actually in the arena, whose face is marred by dust and sweat and blood; who strives valiantly; who errs, who comes short again and again, because there is no effort without error and shortcoming; but who does actually strive to do the deeds; who knows great enthusiasms, the great devotions; who spends himself in a worthy cause; who at the best knows in the end the triumph of high achievement, and who at the worst, if he fails, at least fails while daring greatly, so that his place shall never be with those cold and timid souls who neither know victory nor defeat.*

This determination to embrace what others call "failure" as the learning experiences they are truly intended to be is a major difference between entrepreneurs and followers.

Gambling vs. Risk

Entrepreneurs tend to approach risk in a deliberate and somewhat cautious manner, contrary to popular myth. Entrepreneurs are not gamblers, although the size of risk some are willing to undertake might seem like high-stakes, improbable gambles to non-entrepreneurs.

Risk-taking differs from gambling in several ways:

1. Risk can be analyzed, reduced, measured (internal locus of control), whereas gambling relies upon unexpected change (external locus of control).
2. Risk-taking often leads to improved circumstances. In contrast, gambling produces nothing of value, with a much higher probability of loss. At best, gambling redistributes assets with no net gain to society. Still, more often, gambling creates misery and loss.[1] Entrepreneurial risk-taking can sometimes cause negative personal outcomes,[2] but most situations produce a positive outcome.
3. Risk-taking can provide personal satisfaction of a job well done and help provided to others. Psychologist studies among large lottery winners indicate gambling robs "winners" of any sense of purpose or satisfaction and

---

[1] Crimes and family dysfunction related to gambling addiction, higher cost to non-gamblers for increased police and social worker services, and shifting of personal failures into the public cost.

[2] Loss of savings, environmental damage, employee dislocations, etc.

often leads them back into poverty or injurious personal behaviors. God created us to feel accomplishment from work and calculated risk-taking. Idleness and unearned benefits cause psychological harm by demeaning self-confidence, losing the ability for gratitude, and undermining other aspects of the *Imago Dei*—image of God—ingrained in all humans.

Types of Risk

What are the primary types of risk? For entrepreneurs, we can consider six categories:

1. **Market risk**: Volatility in sales volumes or collections, over-reliance on a narrow customer base.[3] Changing consumer demands (and therefore requiring a change in pricing and marketing strategies, gross profit margins, etc.). And changes in reputation (including branding recognition, public relations, market positioning, etc.)
2. **Strategic risk**: Effects upon your company from industry or technology.[4] Disruptive innovation creates permanent substantial shifts in a product line, consumer demand, profit margins or other key factors that require a major revamp of your business model, and government actions that affect your ability to continue pursuing your

---

[3] Usually defined as any single customer accounting for more than 5 percent of total sales or a particular niche representing greater than 25 percent of total sales.

[4] Narrowing, merging of industries such as the combination of telephone, cable, entertainment and internet industries towards a single industry.

business model.
3. **Compliance risk**: Changes in tax rates, regulatory restrictions, and other government actions either to your own company or to others. This might not necessitate a change in the business model, but it can generate higher risks or changes in procedures, particularly from arbitrary or sudden changes such as a court ruling or new regulation.
4. **Operational risk**: Bottlenecks, changing costs, personnel retraining or other internal aspects, vendor/partner transportation, production scheduling, and similar challenges.
5. **Financial risk**: Liquidity traps, leverage (which can frequently both help and hurt by magnifying results quickly), depreciation in asset values or usefulness, banking requirements, investor expectations and relations, conflicting demands from stakeholder groups, and changes in the value or cost of money.
6. **Human Resource risk**: Hiring mistakes, training and assignment/promotion issues, levels of disclosure among various employees and to selected vendors, independent distributors' or partners' commitment to your company's sales, networking contacts (among other industry players, government leaders, and target prospect groups), intellectual property protection, outsourcing, and artificial intelligence or robotic replacement of local workers and similar people-related issues of feelings and perceptions.

None of these risk categories are insurmountable. Entrepreneurs manage them every day.

Managing Risk Challenges

There is sometimes an overlapping effect among different types of risk, making problem-solving more challenging. By grouping risks among these different categories, you can begin to better analyze and minimize the costs and disruptions which might arise from each type of risk-taking effort. The possibility of not succeeding on the first try is not a sufficient excuse for avoiding making the attempted effort.

Study the proposed transaction to find ways of partially controlling or minimizing the risk of loss. Then make an informed judgment call. Will the probability of success be sufficiently greater than the possibility of loss? If so, make the attempt worth the effort.

If it fails, the correct response is to study why the situation did not work the way you intended and change the variables to improve your probability of success in the next endeavor. Remember, you only fail when you give up. Or worse, don't even start! Failure has nothing to do with repeated attempts or fresh approaches as a result of careful analysis.

That is also why many entrepreneurs use the word "challenges" rather than "problems." Many people tend to view a problem as something external that happens to them, so they must be tolerated or overcome through reaction. In contrast, challenges could be either re-actively or pro-actively recognized, and are inherently mostly an internal locus of control or solvable by the entrepreneur. Therefore, challenges are a positive opportunity to learn and improve the approach. Each attempt that falls short must be a learning experience. Without analysis, you are shifting to a losing, external locus of control mindset.

In this chapter, we've learned that to win as an entrepreneur, your perspective needs to be transformed. You need to assess your risks, and rise to your challenges. In the next chapter, we'll learn about loops, hedgehogs, and innovation.

4

Triple Loop Learning & Design Thinking

Spurring innovation involves learning from the risks you undertake. In this chapter, we will review two theories for promoting maximum learning from your creative thinking efforts. Each of these theories provides varying views to the same general approach, which you can utilize for your employees, vendors, investors, and other stakeholders, and for yourself.

To understand triple loop learning we first need to understand each of the learning loops. **A loop** is a continuous circle or a never-ending review of each step in a process. Each step has to be methodically reviewed to find new insights that might be implemented to improve profitability, have higher quality or consistency, have swifter processing, or other types of gains.

A **single loop learning** system involves correcting deviations from a set of rules management has imposed. The goal is to minimize deviations from those rules, which presumably are the "best" way to accomplish the task at hand. **Double-**

loop learning probes deeper to reflect upon why deviations occurred, then considers whether the rules need to be changed in addition to eliminating deviations.

For example, suppose you own a small fabricated house manufacturing company. For quality control and cash flow purposes, you layout your factory building so raw materials are received on a loading dock at one side of the building, and each step in the process[5] laid out in a straight line ending at the other loading dock on the far side of your factory where the final kits are loaded onto trucks for delivery to work sites. You could establish either one master form per house order or multiple forms that serve as checklists and hand-offs to the crew working the next step.

A single loop learning approach would involve supervisors or a factory manager reviewing each completed form to question any deviations in quality, completeness, excessive wasted materials, or delay in completing each stage. If the manager sees a pattern developing, he or she can focus on the workers, quality of materials, or architectural layout, causing repeated deviations from the most efficient manufacturing processes. Advancing to a double loop learning system would include discussing with workers why such deviations occur, and whether management can track the deviations with fewer interruptions to workers by using a different tracking system.

---

[5] Framing, installing wiring, and plumbing in accordance with one of several standardized architectural designs, insulation and sheetrock added at another stage, trim and paint included in a later step, and discrete markings checked to assure each component will perfectly fit when assembled on the building site.

It would also involve considering whether computerizing the process, by including hand-held scanners for the quantity of material and labor steps completed, would reduce the number of forms completed in each step. Or considering if by changing some other portion of the production line the quality control systems might improve results.

Triple loop learning pushes learning efforts even further. It does this by exploring the process of learning—how to learn more. It involves how and why questions: Why are there deviations in the current system? How can I fix this? At this point, we can also consider asking how and why questions to the rules: Why are these rules not working? How can I change these rules?

Analyze the rules and find potential changes. This proactive thought process provides an opportunity for us to think about how and when to proactively make further changes in a more effective way in the future. This approach has occasionally been called **problem-based learning**—which is described as finding useful information to learn by solving a real-world problem first and considering how to eliminate the problem from occurring, not simply attempting to identify and minimize deviations.

Triple Loop in Action

Utilizing our fabricated housing manufacturer example triple loop learning could lead you to rearrange your plant layout. For example, perhaps some sections which do not require plumbing or wiring might be completed or partially assembled while another crew installs plumbing and wiring. Maybe shingles and roofing structures can be built independently from installing a kitchen sink or toilet, and panels might show plumbing cutouts.

Working in parallel might reduce overall construction time, reduce errors by allowing for smaller more specialized crews, eliminate some tracking forms paperwork, and permit supervisors and managers to invest more time on quality control inspections more frequently. Perhaps in talking with vendors about your operation some might be able to provide partially assembled units instead of just raw materials, further reducing time and possibly saving cash flow.

Deviations

Triple loop learning reinforces a constant feedback of learning about deviations from rules. Deviations can include modifying the current rules: If they are not the best ones to accomplish company goals, change them or throw them out altogether! The entire process of goals, including their creation and modification, should be regularly re-examined in light of constant feedback from the first two loops and a changing external market.

Essentially, adjust targets and expectations according to the ongoing feedback loop from all available sources, and seemingly unending problem-solving that keeps the business going. The key is to not get too attached to any idea or process just for the sake of the idea or process. This can be particularly difficult, as consistency can also be a core business competency. However, in an innovative business, it is more important to embrace the potentially disruptive side of these changes, as they lead to improvements in both idea generation and stable, efficient processes.

Examples

Exceptional success generally comes over time from the deliberate, frequent practice of learning loops. In the book, *Good to Great,* Dr. Jim Collins called this the **Hedgehog Principle**. It takes patience and consistency to instill a company-wide philosophy of constant improvement, but the results can be phenomenal over a longer period.

Another more "nuts and bolts" way to teach triple loop learning is a Japanese concept called kaizen. **Kaizen Events** are a day when companies shut down all normal operations. Managers walk through each step of operations throughout the entire company with employees, identifying unnecessary paperwork or employee actions, cutting wasted time and materials. Every action and form must be justified during a Kaizen Event or it will be eliminated. The result, if accompanied by employee rewards for greater efficiency and assurances that employee jobs eliminated will be re-tasked to other expansion jobs when possible, has resulted in many companies accomplishing huge leaps in productivity after several Kaizen Events.

Another theory to generate greater creativity is called **Design Thinking**. One definition for Design Thinking is a methodology for solving complex problems and discovering optimal solutions utilizing a combination of logic, imagination, intuition, and systemic reasoning. Another way of describing Design Thinking is an exploration of business processes to improve performance. Note the emphasis on the left and the right brain uses to combine free-thinking creative efforts with a logical and systematic effort to improve operational designs and processes by re-imagining them.

Stanford University offers several practical-oriented steps to accomplish a Design Thinking effort. These steps are:

1. Understand all aspects of the process you are modifying. Be familiar with the subject; know it from as many angles as you can think of.
2. Observe your environment. How does this particular process fit into the overall framework of other processes?
3. Seek out alternative points of view on how the process might be accomplished. At this early point, do not be concerned about whether any of those viewpoints seem to make sense or might appear inefficient.
4. Ideate. This is a term describing brainstorming, or letting your imagination roam wild with the data you gathered in prior steps without inhibitions to dream of new possibilities.
5. Build a prototype. This is the stage where those uninhibited ideas and possible alternatives will be winnowed down through the attempt to build a workable model.

6. Tinker and test the model repeatedly, making improvements constantly.

To recap the Design Thinking approach, take five actions:

1. Draw—create a picture or flowchart of what you envision, and ask others to critique it.
2. See—make a collage or photo, put it aside for a short while, then review it to see if you notice flaws or inefficiencies; graphics and pictures can generate more powerful insights than writings or tables of figures.
3. Build—try a quick, simple construction, don't worry about outward attractiveness, perhaps start with a craft store mockup or computer CAD/CAM drawing, then proceeding to an actual working prototype product.
4. Make—map the journey from potential sales and marketing points, to product manufacturing, to customer reasons for satisfaction and repeat sales; some entrepreneurs even act out or chart the start-to-finish business cycles as a way of reviewing whether the proposed product and its related pricing, delivery channels, etc. make sense.
5. Reflect—collect compliments and criticisms, explore the origins of your ideas and enhancements again, show and tell others for their reactions, build a notebook of pluses and minuses that could be improved.

5

Key Learning Practices

What are the eight key learning practices each entrepreneur should encourage among employees and perhaps your vendors?

The first discipline is to **practice deliberative thinking**. While you want your thoughts to explore as wide a range of possibilities as possible, there is still a structure or organization to such efforts. Focus on specific tasks. Reflect upon all the possible ways that tasks might be accomplished or eliminated before moving on to the next one.

Second, **master your domain**. Understand as many aspects of your environment as possible. That might involve coaching or discussing with vendors, employees, customers, and other people their views on the marketplace, company operations, and other components of the situation in which you are competing. Pursue the deepest understanding you can of even peripheral topics, and consider ways to apply your increasing learning to new situations.

Third, **never stop learning**. Seek new knowledge relentlessly and encourage your associates to do likewise. Some entrepreneurs keep notebooks or jot brief insights or new facts into their phones, computers, a small notepad kept in a car or in a jacket pocket. Alongside those new insights, try to customize that knowledge with an idea or two of how it might be applied to your business, even if the idea seems impractical at first.

Read. Read deeply. Read widely. Read books and magazines on a wide variety of topics, not solely those related to your business or to your personal interests. Many of the most successful entrepreneurs are voracious readers, and always open to hearing new ideas at any time from any source. Another method for assuring continuous learning is to recruit one or more mentors who can regularly challenge you to expand your horizons, including reading recommendations.

The fourth key learning practice involves **balancing high specialization with becoming a generalist**. That is not necessarily a contradiction in terms. As noted earlier, you should seek to master your domain by gaining a very deep understanding of your chosen field of expertise. Yet, there may be developments in fields that seem unrelated to yours which could offer new opportunities for you.

Picture your learning efforts as a cross. The main post digs deep into your business field of expertise. Yet the wider you stretch to learn a bit about many other fields, the greater the probability that you will eventually discover ideas that can be applied in unconventional or creative manners to help your business. In the positive sense of the word, you should become a dilettante, an amateur in exploring other fields of knowledge outside your area of expertise arising from casual or superficial interest. If an area of knowledge ignites your interest then you might consider pairing with an expert in that field or interviewing someone with extensive understanding of that area.

Fifth, **visualize applications for the new knowledge you obtain**. Try not to leave it in the form of disconnected, abstract information. When we attempt to visualize possible uses for new ideas (or new uses for old ideas) this effort can stimulate more innovation and further the triple loop learning process.

Sixth, **relax and take breaks**. Bursts of concentration can lead to new insights, but there is validity in clearing your mind by turning to another task or doing something physical such as taking a walk. Eventually, your thoughts will return to the information you were gathering or the situation you were pondering, and your mind will generate new angles to consider.

Many inventors claim a large number of their breakthrough ideas come to them when they relax and clear their minds of the blockage they have struggled with. There is a reason thinking of new ideas in the shower is a cliché! We were created by God as creatures designed for work, but also for rest. Even God rested after the big brainstorming session of the creation of the universe! Incorporate the habit of scheduled rest into your routine. Some entrepreneurs work best in spurts rather than constant plodding.

Seventh, **find the right framework or box to view the challenge**. Sometimes we need to look at a situation from a different viewpoint. Remember John Rockefeller's very different framing of the oil pollution issue farmers were so frustrated about? Ask yourself how a cost might actually be considered a benefit. How could a process be restructured to avoid a roadblock? When you need to look at a situation from a different perspective, it is sometimes best to do so through somebody else's eyes. Do not hesitate to ask people you trust to explore out loud other ways they could consider the situation or accomplish the same task using different resources.

Finally, **become a beginner**. By this, I mean to question the assumptions that you think you "know" have always been right or that what you were taught is the "correct" way of tackling a challenge. Be humble. Perhaps what you and everyone else "knows" might be wrong. Stanley Tam[6] provides an interesting example:

He nearly went bankrupt trying to recover the silver from used photography studios. After arriving at the brink of insolvency, he re-imagined the basic premise of his business model, considering with fresh "beginner" eyes how the silver could be recovered? His competitors had tried and failed, leading to only very small businesses able to recover very

---

[6] To learn more about this, read my book Transforming Entrepreneurs

limited amounts within a small geographic area of their shops. But they didn't view things with a beginner's eyes like Stanley.

Stanley thought about reversing the industry model to send out recovery bottles and packages, asking photo studios to send him the materials rather than picking them up from each location. The result was a multi-million dollar business during a depressed business climate. All because Stanley was willing to humbly question everything he and his competitors thought they knew about their own businesses.

The old maxim is often (though not always) true that more heads are more valuable than one. Involve others in your discoveries, whether customers, employees, suppliers, or others. Obviously, there is a limit to how much you can safely share while avoiding the risk of someone sharing your ideas with a competitor or becoming a new competitor. But there is value in asking others to consider aspects of your ideas from their own viewpoints. Building upon both the theories of Triple Loop Learning and Design Thinking, you can create greater probabilities for discovering innovative ideas.

Add to these theories one important additional idea. Our God is very creative. He made us in His image, which includes the innate ability to be innovative and utilize our reasoning minds to explore this world and to רָמַשׁ (Hebrew word translated as "to keep, guard, observe, give heed, have charge of, protect" from Genesis 2:15). Therefore it stands to reason that praying for guidance, as many scientists have done, such as Blaise Pascal, Sir Isacc Newton, Johannes Kepler, and others as well as many Christian entrepreneurs have done, is also an important aspect of innovation to pursue.

6

Protecting Your Ideas

Ideas are precious commodities. While it may be surprising to some, taking appropriate precautions to protect your creative ideas can sometimes open up new avenues to greater innovation. In addition, legal protections not only safeguards you and your company, but also improves your chances of generating sufficient revenue to fund additional new insights. In other words, protecting company intellectual property rights is part of increasing your ability to "be fruitful" as faithful stewards of the resources God is giving us.

Non-Disclosure Agreements

Non-disclosure agreements are perhaps the initial point where many inventors begin protecting their ideas. A **non-disclosure agreement** is what it sounds like. The entrepreneur asks a potential investor, vendor, employee, or another possible stakeholder to sign a formal legal agreement not to disclose what you are about to share with them in exchange for some right or benefit. Often the penalties are specified in monetary terms, and sometimes as a "cease or desist" default court order if the agreement is violated.

The idea is to encourage collaboration without fear of theft. The other party signing such an agreement is prohibited from using either any government-licensed monopoly information (which I will describe later in this chapter) or trade secrets to generate revenue for anyone other than your company. The concept is to create a right of compensation for any damage to intellectual property you created with your innovations. In many nations, this type of agreement can be enforced in an absolute manner. However, in the United States, non-disclosure agreements are limited in duration, scope, geographic reach, or even void with respect to any data previously released into the public domain and other limitations imposed by each state.

Non-Compete Agreement

Another common type of legal agreement is a **non-compete agreement**. Employees usually request this type of agreement as a condition of hire. It is also occasionally used with key vendors providing critical goods or services.

Like the non-disclosure agreement,[7] a non-compete agreement attempts to prohibit or limit an employee's ability to take customers, innovative ideas or processes, or other valuable intangible assets from your company without paying

---

[7] Often incorporated into the non-compete agreement.

the penalty.

This type of agreement can be enforced with few to no restrictions in many nations, but is frequently limited in the United States due to the 13th Amendment to the Constitution, which prohibits "involuntary servitude." Courts have placed time and geography limits and have sometimes prohibited bans against servicing unsolicited business. To do so would be interpreted as the equivalent of forcing an ex-employee to work for you for free or against his or her will. Nonetheless, this type of agreement can give ex-employees pause to consider competing against you with your own ideas, if for no other reason than the high cost of litigation in nearly any American court.

Monopoly Rights

Governments grant special monopoly rights for some time to inventors to encourage them to develop more societal improvements. The lowest cost monopoly grant is for written materials. A **copyright** gives the writer control over the use and distribution of an original work. Registration is low-cost, quick, and easy in most nations. It gives you the right to sue others when they use your copyrighted materials. The government will not help you enforce this right. It simply recognizes the property is yours, which can help in a court action and can intimidate a violator into making a financial settlement with you after you catch them. Copyrights can include not only books and marketing materials but also software code.

Trademarks are another type of government-granted special monopoly right which you can purchase cheaply and swiftly. Trademarks can involve symbols, words, or graphics unique to your company (if you are the first to file for it). Trademarks can be reserved at the county level with your county clerk, state level with a Secretary of State, or reserved with a foreign national commercial registry office. That gives you the right to sue others when they use your trademark. The idea is to prevent unscrupulous merchants from stealing your goodwill and credibility to market their "knockoff" products while deceptively portraying themselves as somehow being allowed to borrow your hard-earned market credibility.

A much more expensive government grant is called a **patent**. This license confers a monopoly right or title for a set period to the first person to file for a new invention. Again, the government will not enforce this privilege for you. It just gives you a preference in court for establishing that you are the first and rightful inventor of the idea.

Another protection is called a **trade secret**. Trade secrets involve a formula, practice, process, design, instrument, pattern, commercial method, or other critical company information not known or reasonably ascertainable by others outside your company. That can be difficult to establish in a courtroom, and it does not involve filing for a government monopoly license. The huge drawback to the various government monopoly grants is the requirement to fully disclose all the information on your idea. Trade secrets are just that – secrets kept within your own company. For example, Coca-Cola has kept its syrup mix a trade secret for over a century.

Royalties and Licensing

Having covered the various ways you can protect your inventions and creative ideas, you should understand one additional protective idea. **Royalties** involve your company licensing your ideas to selected other companies in exchange for a fee, usually calculated as a percentage of the other company's revenue on all products or services they sell involving the use of your idea. A royalty agreement can enable the expansion of your creative ideas or provide a lower cost, non-lawsuit approach to working with other companies and sharing each others' ideas when there is some synergy or overlap.

All of these methods are designed to work to the benefit of the entrepreneur. They are designed to foster business by ensuring the risk and reward calculation is sufficient for an entrepreneur to get their business off the ground. When considering legal protection, all of these are possible forms of legal protection to consider. Some are better suited to specific forms of entrepreneurial businesses. When considering legal protections, if possible, research and then consult with an attorney to ensure that protections are properly set up in the jurisdiction in which your business operates.

II

Marketing

Marketing looks at how to convey your message about what you are offering and common principles in making and completing actual sales.

Chapter 7 explores how to test viability.

Chapter 8 teaches you how to advertise and promote your business via social media.

Chapter 9 explores the sales cycle or process.

Chapter 10 focuses on strategies and distribution channels.

7

Testing Viability

Wouldn't it be great if you simply rented a storefront or office space and customers immediately began flooding in to purchase your product and service offerings? That only happens in fantasy movies. In real life, many startup businesses fail because they spend too much money initially without generating sufficient revenue—or, in some cases, any revenue at all.

Testing the Market

You can increase your survival odds substantially by test marketing sample offerings to gauge marketplace interest conducting other tests. It is also important to pivot to a modified or new business model when testing indicates you are unlikely to generate sufficient sales to reach a breakeven point prior to running out of cash. Uncovering the amount of demand can be done fast and cheaply, although only on an approximate rather than an accurate basis.

The obvious place to start is with a **survey** of potential customers. To prepare a good survey, conduct research on the industry and niche dollar and product volume size for the type of business you are contemplating. Also, check with your local Chamber of Commerce for similar local data, particularly street traffic volumes, if you are considering opening a retail store. Determine how many competitors are already offering the same or similar products or services, and obtain samples of their marketing materials. After this initial "desk research" effort, you should be knowledgeable enough to create your initial survey.

The initial survey of random prospects should include no more than ten questions. The first several should include basic demographic questions but not names or personal identifying information. The two-fold purpose for demographic questions is to see if any common characteristics might help predict which people would be interested in your product or service. The other purpose is to build rapport and comfort to encourage interviewees to respond to more personal questions. Additional questions can ask about desired product features, price ranges a prospect might be willing to pay, level of customer support expected, and delivery time if not received immediately.

Don't shy away from the price question and make a reasonable estimate of several ranges where you can afford to produce the product and make various profit levels. Nearly everyone is willing to consider buying a product at an unspecified price, but stating several price ranges will quickly help you determine if you can meet customer expectations and still make a profit.

Generally, a sample of 200 people chosen randomly from brief street interviews or trade associations will give you sufficient information to determine customer expectations. Then you can begin designing your product or service and exploring what your operating costs might look like to figure whether you can produce and deliver your idea profitably.

Applying Survey Results in Action

Survey results can help you determine market niches you might capture. For example, one of my clients ran a small, struggling car repair shop specializing in Volvo vehicles, a relatively expensive car to purchase and maintain or repair. I helped him design a brief survey which he asked each customer to complete. After a few months of using the survey, we analyzed the results. Customers indicated they tend to be younger (under 35) with white-collar office jobs but do not like to join any associations or have common interests. But many had young elementary school children, most of whom attended one particular neighborhood school. I suggested that the business owner volunteer to help that school's PTA (Parent-Teacher Association) organize some of their fund-raising activities.

Within a year, we could attribute a 30% increase in his sales and a growing number of repeat customers in exchange for the approximately three hours per month of evening volunteer time and the positive publicity it brought to his business. Over a two-year period, his profits (not just revenues) rose nearly $200,000 annually. Not bad for an initially one-person car repair shop!

The point is to get a feel for the demand before you sink a large amount of money into a new enterprise that might fail if not structured properly to meet the real demand cost-effectively. However, surveys are not foolproof. As an old small business saying states, no business plan survives first contact with customers. Thus we need to contemplate utilizing two other market planning approaches.

Test Ads

Some entrepreneurs have utilized online test ads offering a mock product or service. Using this approach, you should market and sell as a pre-order approach. The product or service will be available within some reasonable period in the future that you think you can provide it in at least smaller quantities. A good example of this approach is the online strategy games seller Steam. Game developers pre-sell concepts before the game is completed, and they modify the games based upon solicited input from people entering reservations for the games. In other words, interested potential customers help provide design specifics that can help attract additional future customers.

Responding to Customer Feedback

Steam game developers also illustrate the second approach: quick changes in response to customer feedback as the product offering is initially rolled out to the public. For example, Steam game developers offer steeply discounted "alpha" stage versions of games that may lack polished graphics in exchange for gathering feedback from hardcore gamers on which features need to be added, subtracted, or modified.

When a major set of improvements are completed and the graphics reach sufficiently high quality to market to the general public, game developers then offer a higher but still significantly discounted "beta" phase version for avid gamers to play in exchange for more feedback. By the time the game is opened to the general public at full price, it has been modified a number of times and tested by actual game players (not just the obviously biased team of developers).

The continuous improvement approach can be more challenging since too much change can make a game seem too unstable to purchase but can help produce a highly marketable product.

Fast decision-making and a short cycle time between new versions of your product or service emphasize the speed in adaptation. *As a startup company, your ability to acclimate swiftly to marketplace demands gives you a huge advantage over large companies tied down by bureaucratic internal approval processes.*

Self-confidence in your research and ability to respond expeditiously is a significant strength for entrepreneurs. If you are afraid to fail in the startup phase, then you are destined to do so at some point. Design experiments to test and validate your hypotheses about what customers are willing to pay for, and continue to test as you grow your company since potential customers' expectations will change over time. A Biblical-centered approach to designing your product or service should always center on solving customer needs first. After that, you can back into the product features required to do so.

Solving Customer Needs

Finally, build upon that basic value proposition with minimal cost and quick adaptation to arrive at a business model likely to be viable over the long term. The United States Small Business Administration cites several reasons for the high failure rate among businesses during their first five years, such as insufficient capitalization. But the main reason is poor management.

We will discuss controlling operations and cash flow in future chapters, but most managerial failure derives from an inward focus on profits, cash flow, and other internal desires. Instead, you increase your probability of success by caring about meeting the needs of potential customers first – an external focus. Most people purchase services to solve a problem. The emotional need they are trying to meet is either desire or fear. Of these two emotions, fear is the more motivational for most people. If you design your offering to meet their needs, some customers will usually help promote your product or service to others.

TESTING VIABILITY

Your initial survey research should point you towards exploring one of five marketing approaches to help solve potential customers' needs. These five approaches are:

1. New product or service introduced into an existing market.
2. New product or service creating a new market niche.
3. New product or service repositioned as a low-cost entrant.
4. Modified product or service targeted to serve as a niche entrant into a narrow market.
5. Copying a successful model into a large market.[8]

When refining your product or service offering, your research should continue to clarify which avenues provide quick, steady (or at least seasonal), and growing sales. In other words, which avenues appear to be the most likely to return a good investment for your marketing and sales efforts and for the dollars you've invested. This continuing analysis can help you identify the better distribution channel choices to fit the pricing, customer types or profiles, customer demands, margins for value-added resellers, complexity for selling your offerings, customer buying habits, segment niches who might be interested in your offerings, and similar research issues.

---

[8] This eventually leads to a low-cost provider approach

Customer Expectations

When testing the viability of your idea, you are probably aware you will be unable to meet all potential customers' expectations and possibly not even stand out as attractive enough to a significant portion of them. As long as those who do see value in your offering generate a sustainable profit level, you have enough justification for launching your new enterprise. There will be trade-offs for customer needs, product performance, competition strengths versus yours, risk, etc.

Competitors

Develop an objective look at your competitors. A well-established approach to this is to summarize all major competitors in a **SWOT box**. The four boxes in the SWOT diagram are labeled Strengths, Weaknesses, Opportunities, and Threats. Every competitor has all four of these. Suppose you can design your offering to avoid directly competing against your competitors' strengths and find opportunities to fulfill gaps in their offerings. In that case, you increase your company's feasibility of long-term success.

Nonprofit Organizations

If you are starting a non-profit organization that will be heavily dependent upon donations rather than sales, you have additional considerations to determine viability. Such nonprofits separate customers from revenue, unlike for-profit businesses. Thus, this approach requires two separate sets of surveys and research efforts, particularly emphasizing what might motivate potential donors. What communications content and frequency would keep donors engaged? Can you leverage sales or creative giving strategies to fund general overhead (which most donors are reluctant to fund)?

Nonprofits can explore **mixed revenue models**. For example, a mental health clinic might charge a small or sliding scale amount per visit based upon the patient's income and soliciting donors to fund the deficit. Many Christian schools charge tuition but also build scholarship or endowment funds to offer subsidized or free tuition to poorer children.

A highly entrepreneurial Christian social services charity in the Houston, Texas area, asks beneficiaries of free food, housing, counseling, and other services to provide free labor gathering food and other product donations from area residents and businesses, as well as assisting in operating the stores that work similarly to Goodwill Industries, Industries for the Blind, and Habitat for Humanity's Restores.

When researching a mixed model approach, you may find some recipients of welfare services and goods might be unwilling to contribute time towards helping themselves. At the same time, some potential donors might expect some recipient "show of appreciation" before volunteering time and money. It is obviously important to learn what combination of product or service provision and donor solicitation could become a sustainable model for your idea.

A brief note: Not all non-profit organizations should conduct two types of surveys to build a successful business model. It is not always necessary. For example, a good friend of mine built a hospital in a developing nation serving middle-class people in a city. He applies the profits towards subsidizing medical services among poor people in rural areas. This charity model is self-sustaining entirely from sales. Any donations fund the startup phase and occasional expansions of buildings and equipment. In this example, the middle-class city dwellers are the only ones necessary to survey before commencing operations. The demand for free medical services among the rural poor is not only obvious but also well documented by government agencies.

Each entrepreneur will need to consider one of these methods of testing viability for their specific business plan, although it will vary based upon the area of interest. Surveys, testing phases, and market data will contribute to the effectiveness of your business plan and the overall success and survivability of the business. After all, failure to plan is ensuring that the plan will fail.[9]

---

[9] A pithy phrase attributed to Benjamin Franklin.

8

Advertising & Social Media

Exposure among potential customers is always the responsibility of the entrepreneur. Advertising can both convey information that hopefully generates interest (marketing) and spark the desire to purchase (sales). Advertising products and services that attempt to create a new industry or niche might be far more expensive than promoting a similar offering in a well-established marketplace. Still, the approach to building an effective marketing campaign is the same.

Sell the Sizzle

When advertising there is no need to detail all the "who, what, when, where, why, how?" series of questions. As a famous marketing genius, Zig Ziglar stated many times, "Sell the sizzle, not the steak!" Customers are interested in solutions that solve problems; they buy offerings that meet a need. The product or service features are somewhat important, but potential customers do not express interest in such details until late in the sales process—and sometimes not at all. Advertising should reflect the understanding of your research into customer needs and then concisely state how your product or service fills those needs.

An Example

Startup companies can most effectively convey their messages to the widest number of potential customers utilizing guerrilla marketing techniques to make up for the lower amount of money available to them in the early stages of development. Earned media —versus paid media coverage—is a good illustration. For example, one of my clients was a startup, a high-quality titanium golf club manufacturer. He struggled to slowly build his sales from a small, low-cost manufacturing facility in an out-of-the-way location. I helped him put together a free event at an inner-city public golf course for lower-income children.

The event featured a variety of his child-sized golf clubs,[10] a local golf pro who agreed to provide free lessons in exchange for media publicity, a local fast food restaurant owner who donated hot dogs and drinks,[11] plus a nearby novelty store's balloons. My client contacted all the local newspapers, radio

---

[10] Made from scrap metal pieces left over after manufacturing adult-sized clubs.

[11] Along with his restaurant's large banner showing the restaurant name and location.

stations, and television outlets in the area. He also invited local politicians to make brief statements of support in front of the reporters. And finally, the local elementary and middle school principals were invited along with their students. The cost to my client was negligible, but the publicity increased his sales by greater than 35% over the next year. Later that year, he was also invited to a dinner meeting at one of the wealthiest country clubs in the city to talk about his innovative charitable efforts. Attending the meeting were many affluent and sympathetic club members who also happened to be the ideal demographic for becoming potential customers.

Other Forms of Advertisement

There is no such thing as free media coverage. However, there can be coverage earned by doing something newsworthy rather than paying cash. Such earned media can never fully replace paid media, but it can provide a low-cost or free boost to a new company's exposure. Other types of low-cost—but sometimes high-time commitment advertising are blogs, tweets, websites, loyalty programs to reward referring and repeat customers, and similar efforts to place customer appreciation foremost.

Customer surveys can accomplish multiple goals. Surveys can tell you about changing customer tastes, as we discussed in a previous chapter. They can also obtain reactions on product improvements, new cross-selling opportunities, and similar items you are preparing to launch.

Your company will generate a greater and gradually growing response rate when applying a wide variety of modes to advertise your message. Internet-based approaches such as a website, pay-per-click campaigns, and viral marketing with embedded incentives are one type of promotional channel. Incidentally, you can keep the sometimes high cost of pay-per-click to an affordable level by buying common misspellings, words, or phrases that have a fair number of searches but are too focused for high-spending competitors to choose such narrow demographics. You can also combine local city or area names with a product type or industry.

Do not overlook old-fashioned modes of advertising, such as paper mailings, radio, or television ads.[12] In all industries, your best and easiest customer to sell is a repeat customer. Find ways to stay in touch regularly, such as a newsletter, new services, and product announcements, customer appreciation days, and similar excuses to maintain relationships without becoming overwhelming or boring by saying the same thing in the same way via the same media every time. In general, your goal should be to contact each prospect or customer at least seven times using seven different modes of contact each year.

The frequency may vary, depending upon your industry, however marketing research indicates potential customers do not begin to recognize or pay any attention to your products or services until they hear from you at least seven times.

---

[12] They can be produced cheaply, and many stations sell "filler" spots at surprisingly low prices, particularly cable channels.

Advertising has several rules that violate what you learned in school to be a good student: 99% wrong can be an A+ since it takes so much contact to gain traction in potential customers' minds. So an initial 1% response rate is not uncommon. The more face-to-face contact you generate, the greater the response rate to your advertising campaign—even if you are an online business.

Potential customers are not your high school English teacher, so you do not need to write advertising literature in full sentences. Bullet points and a significant amount of blank space will actually prompt more people to read your advertising than will clutter, complete sentences, and paragraphs.

It is vital to monitor advertising effectiveness. Online advertising can trace sources easily through search engine optimization, email responses to viral marketing, autoresponders (automated standard email messages). Even with paper mailings can be source traced by offering some discount or deal if the responder repeats back to you the code printed on the mailing. Over time, common patterns will emerge. Certain wording will generate greater interest, as will certain modes of communication or particular times of the year. Reinforce the higher response-generating approaches and cut back or eliminate those that are unproductive.

Marketing as Christian

Make marketing content appropriate and attractive to the target audience in the mode they most prefer. Certainly, you should experiment with supplemental modes of communication to reinforce the awareness of your message, but focus most of your advertising budget and efforts on those promotional efforts that generate the most return for your investment. Always try to maintain a friendly and respectful tone to your advertising in keeping with the Biblical ideal of serving others.

For example, use permission email lists to avoid annoying people with "junk mailings." Make the unsubscribe button easy to find, and always allow an opportunity for individuals to give feedback as to why they hit the unsubscribe button. Any lukewarm responses you receive are an indication of a problem. Before it can become a significant problem, follow up to find out why customers or prospects are not enthusiastic about what your company is offering to them.

Whether organized as for-profit or non-profit, a Christian enterprise's advertising and social media messages can have an educational aspect beyond mere product and service offerings. The Great Commission calls all Christians to share the Gospel's good news with everyone. The most effective way to accomplish this goal has always been to first establish a good personal relationship with someone who comes to trust and value your advice. Impersonal emails are rarely the best way to share the Biblical message, although some Christian entrepreneurs include tracts or pay for mass advertising. Others may take a more low-key approach by sponsoring missions and other charities or displaying a Christian symbol in the corner of their advertising, packaging, or company logo.

The most proven effective method of promoting the Gospel

is one-on-one personal relationship development, not mass advertising. Some advertising can cause people to inquire about your company and personal values or beliefs. The effectiveness of such advertising can vary greatly, depending upon which part of the nation or world your business is located in. In an increasingly less-hospitable culture, your most effective return on time invested in witnessing will be personal interactions with employees foremost, then vendors and customers.

9

Sales

Completing sales and collecting cash is usually the most difficult part of operating a business. Whether utilizing a website, postcards or other mailings, viral marketing emails, cold calling forms, or any other data capture method, the starting point is the same: Gather as much information as possible.

Gathering Customer Information

This may include name, physical address, phone, social media names, email address, etc. Get as much information as the prospect is willing to provide—without pushing them to the point where they shut you out entirely. Gathering enough information to understand what your prospects need and multiple ways to contact them will most likely require a series of varied contacts. There are many contact management software packages, both downloadable and in the cloud, which you can use to keep your notes organized. Old fashioned notebooks and paper also work. Include each date and time of day you contact each prospect and any comments the potential customer mentions, or any products or services they purchase from you.

Offering free trials, particularly with software products or a service, can boost conversion rates from prospects to actual paying customers. Most small businesses now have websites. Hosting services allow you to save email lists in databases that you can sort through by identifying repeat customers or cross-selling possibilities for particular products, prospects interested in solving a particular need, etc. Then, using autoresponders you can automatically send out **email blasts**—mass marketing of your message—with links back to particular **landing pages** featuring the products or services you are promoting at this time. Today websites and autoresponders are an essential minimum sales effort. Surprisingly, many smaller businesses and nonprofit organizations still have not utilized these basic tools.

Hosting services often offer tracking software that shows you which pages or products prospects and customers were looking at, on which days and at which times, and the path they followed moving through your website. Likewise, viral marketing pieces can have embedded links to specific offerings, coupons to print or scan to a phone, and other tracking codes. Create a logical system of codes to include in all print and email advertising. If you ask a customer to key in or scan a code from a printed mailing or mentioned in a radio or video/television ad, you can increase the possibility of making a sale by offering a small discount.

Perhaps a somewhat better sales effort is to offer a discount to any existing customer whose friend uses the original customer's tracking code to make a purchase. You might even consider the same incentive for repeat sales from existing customers. After making a sale you and your staff should make either a personal thank you (such as at a retail outlet) or a personal phone call and other personalized contacts (a technique utilized by wholesalers, manufacturing businesses, and luxury retailers). The goal of this "after-sale" effort is to boost customer satisfaction with your company by building a brand name, not just selling a product, and reinforce retention of customers. Making a repeat sale to a satisfied customer is substantially cheaper than finding a new one. Repeat sales also tend to increase customer loyalty.

Transforming Price Setting

How should you set your pricing? Allow me to digress for a minute into a lesson on basic economic theory: Classical and Keynesian economic theories look at **industry averages**. With a quick Google search, you can find: the listing of gross profit margins, percent of the sale price for each main type of expense, and other data organized by both industry and category of company size. Companies such as **Dun & Bradstreet** publish these guides annually, in print and digital copies. In case you are not familiar with the term, the gross profit margin is the percentage profit earned before any overhead or administrative type expenses. The gross profit is sales revenue minus the direct cost of the goods sold. The margin is calculated as gross profit divided by sales. Many businesses, both large and small, tend to stick to their industry gross profit average.

There is a third school of economic theory not taught often enough in college economic programs, called **Austrian economic theory**. The Austrian model posits that the sales price should be what the market is willing to pay, unrelated to the cost of producing the product or service, and unrelated to any overhead expenses. The business owner should look at what competitors are selling for and what customers tell you they are willing to pay, then compare that price or range to what you project it will cost you to offer the product or service. If the result is sufficiently positive for you to fund your personal needs then the venture should use that price average you discovered with customers.

However, if the result is negative, that says you will not be able to produce your envisioned products at a price customers are willing to buy. The Austrian economic theory offers greater potential if you are willing to make an extra effort to uncover the key variables unlocking greater gross profit. Such variables can include niche uniqueness, the amount of competitive marketplace pricing, local variations, amount of post-selling support, timing, or add-on fees such as shipping and processing costs or warranties fees.

A good example of an Austrian economics pricing model in action is the online TurboTax tax preparation product, offered by Intuit. Intuit offers greater discounts in early January at the beginning of the tax filing season in hopes of aggressively capturing the early filers, who tend to be the most simple returns with refunds, before those prospects can see competing tax services opening up around their areas. As the season progresses, and the procrastinators with more complex returns and taxes owed think about completing their tax returns, Intuit keeps raising the price until the big April 15th deadline, assuming many of these late filers will ask for heavier professional advice on complicated tax issues.

Most competing tax services stick with a blanket industry average gross profit margin throughout the entire season (the Classical and Keynesian models), even as stress and strain (and overtime costs) on firm resources mount up to the filing deadline peak. Intuit's Austrian pricing model helps the company afford to provide greater resources for customers needing higher level and more time-consuming help.

Sales Force Staffing

We will cover staffing in the next section of this book under Operations, but let's take a quick look at the question of sales force staffing. If you are operating an internet-based business your sales force can be (but not necessarily is) robotic. Yet nearly all businesses, including internet companies, need actual salespeople, especially their top salesperson - you, the founder. Good quality sales personnel rarely work on straight commission initially, although as they build contacts and sales top salespeople prefer to move to either a base salary plus commission or straight commission.

You must plan on paying a salary or guaranteed minimum draw against commissions initially, since it typically takes months or a couple of years, depending upon the product or service sold, to build a revenue stream the salesperson can live on. In many companies, the sales staff are the highest earners. They generate the cash stream that enables you to pay everyone else and yourself. Salespeople also need an expense budget for travel, entertainment, and meals for potential customers, sales literature, and some discretion to offer a discounted price (within parameters you set) to win sales in the most competitive situations.

Nonprofit Organizations

Lest you think otherwise, if you are starting a nonprofit organization rather than a for-profit business, you still need sales staff. Nonprofit organizations need all the same overhead structure as for-profit businesses, they simply use different terminology to describe those people. For example, where a for-profit business refers to its front-line sales revenue generating staff as salespeople, nonprofit organizations call them development directors generating donation revenue. The sales pitch and terminology vary, but the activity is very similar.

Sales Cycle Pipeline

What is the actual sales cycle within a business? I've taken a different approach than others when it comes to the sales cycle pipeline. Picture it as the pipeline I created for you in the figure below. You and your sales staff must enter lots of time into the beginning of the pipeline at the bottom in hopes that a portion of that effort will pour out of the spigot at the top as dollars. And yes, it does flow against gravity from bottom to top, just as the sales cycle effort requires a substantial effort to push time, persistence, creativity, active listening ability, and other sales skills uphill against frequent feelings of discouragement to achieve sales from the faucet. *Pay close attention to the parts on the diagram marked with water droplets.* Those are the potential leaks in your pipeline! These are places where you can lose sales. Let's walk through the sales cycle pipeline together.

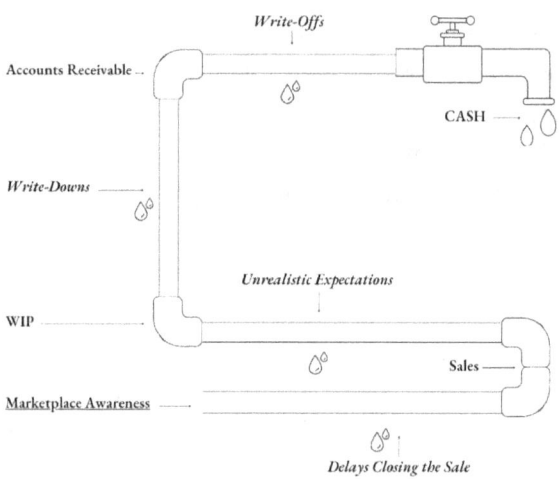

Marketplace Awareness

We begin at the lower-left corner of the diagram: **Marketplace awareness**. We must pour time and money into the funnel at the beginning of the pipeline to create marketplace awareness of your new products and services offerings. This can include the cost of printing brochures, buying ad words on social media, producing and broadcasting radio and television advertisements, and many other forms of messaging. Certainly, the majority of marketing and sales efforts for nearly all successful startups must involve large amounts of time informing prospective customers and listening to their needs. The more innovative your product or service is (especially if attempting to create a new industry or niche) the greater the length of time as well as the lag between beginning to inform and educate consumers before becoming able to make a sale.

Delays Closing the Sale

This is our first potential leak. Note the water droplets under **Delays Closing the Sale.** Economic conditions, insufficient exposure, not having a Unique Selling Proposition, marketing not matching Porter's marketplace position, and inconsistent exposure are some of the ways your time and effort can get clogged and create a leak here in the initial pipe.

For example, if you are selling luxury or recreational goods when the economy dips, it will take many more contacts to find customers still willing to spend money on non-essential products. Each industry also experiences peaks and valleys for demand. An extreme example is swimming pool maintenance contracts or Christmas decoration stores, where an overwhelming amount of sales are made in only one quarter of the year.

In case you are wondering about the reference to Porter's marketplace positioning, this is a model developed by Harvard professor Michale E. Porter in 1979 to help business executives and owners with positioning their offerings in the marketplace. Porter's Five Forces are:

1. **Competition within the industry** – number, quality, and other differences as well as the cost to customers for switching companies

1. **Ease of entry for new participants** – licensing and high cost of facilities or other entrance helps prevent you from being swamped with cheap knockoffs, while low hurdles to entry invite new competitors to quickly skim your hard-fought customers and sales

1. **Buyer Power** – number of customers, size of typical orders, price sensitivity, ability to substitute other products, and similar characteristics that give either customers or your company an advantage in arriving at a balance between supply and demand

1. **Seller Power** (also called **Supplier Power**) – similar to Buyer Power, this aspect reflects the amount of leverage your suppliers have over you. If the parts or product you sell is supplied by a limited number of companies, they can increase prices or cramp your cash flow without warning, while a large number of supplier sources give you more power to dictate terms to the suppliers you purchase from, allowing for improved margins and cash timing

1. **Threats from substitutes** – customers may seek substitute products or services if your prices are perceived as too high and the cost and quality of substitutes are not prohibitive

When considering these five forces affecting your sales ability, your company should emphasize an appropriate corresponding **sales strategy**. The commonly understood sales strategies in response to each force are:

1. Low-cost provider
2. Differentiation (luxury or prestigious image, superior service, early issuance of new products or improved features, etc.)
3. Narrow market niche (such as families, gamers, people living within a certain area, etc.)
4. Integrated (a combined blend of price with added value)

The first pipe in this pipeline is the longest period for every company or organization.

Sale

At some point, a portion of your efforts will begin to pay off as **sales**. This is reflected in the diagram as the first bend in the pipeline. Depending upon the industry you are in, the sale can still be a long time away from realizing the actual cash. This is especially true in **business-to-business (B2B) sales**, such as wholesalers and manufacturers selling to retailers or other companies. Getting an order for a sale and delivering the product does not necessarily generate quick cash or even a stable price.

Unrealistic Expectations

That brings us to our next potential leak: **Unrealistic Expectations**. These leaks may include impossible delivery deadlines, sales staff offering an excessively aggressive discount when not necessary to get the order, customers attempting to utilize their buying power when placing large orders to cut your price or attempting to make you wait a long time to receive payment.

If you are selling to other businesses, understand the concept of **Just In Time (JIT)**. JIT is applied by many larger companies with substantial buying power to demand that a supplier spend its own money building an inventory of product to be supplied as the customer receives orders, thus shifting the cost of funds tied up in inventory to suppliers. This sounds great if you can get your customers to stock your inventory for you at their expense and deliver it nearly immediately after you make a sale, thus allowing you to keep your customers satisfied while not needing to stock any inventory yourself. The flip side to this arrangement is if one or more of your key customers are shifting their inventory costs to you.

Work in Process (WIP)

After advancing through the first two pipe lengths while springing as few leaks as possible we reach **Work in Progress (WIP)**. If you are in the type of business where you provide customized or semi-customized products (such as commercial trucks or computer systems built with specific features, colors, etc.) then you might obtain a deposit from your customer from which you pay for the parts you must purchase to complete the order, often supplemented with loaned money from a bank line of credit.

To complete the order and bill the entire sales amount you must completely execute your part of the sales contract. If there is a significant amount of lag time some customers might decide to change the terms of the project but may be unwilling to pay for the extra work or parts. This can be a common situation with consulting contracts. Thus the WIP bend in the pipeline can create a clog towards getting paid.

Write-Downs

Our next leakage area is **write-downs**. Even though your company fulfills your part of the sales contract, some customers may cause more leaks in the sales collection cycle by complaining about the quality of work or product, creating inefficiencies via too many changes in specifications and other quality-related complaints, or simply try to use buyer power to change the deal after agreeing to terms when you are too deep into completing your end of the contract to pull out without suffering a significant loss. Good customer management combined with a carefully crafted sales contract can minimize leakage between WIP and delivery of the end product or service.

Accounts Receivable

The final bend in the sales cycle pipeline is **accounts receivable**. Your company delivered the product or service and sent an invoice with terms specifying the due date by which the payment is due. You now have an account receivable. But the sales challenge is not yet over. Our last area where many companies frequently spring leaks in the sales cycle is write-offs of some or all of a receivable (as opposed to a write-down of the sale price during the WIP phase). Write-offs can be caused by a customer with high buyer power demanding discounts or threatening to take future sales to competitors, or from a customer's inability to pay.

Efforts to collect can themselves cause delays and create

additional costs, such as filing in small claims court, working out a payment plan, hiring a collections agency, using a factoring company (which involves selling your receivable to a finance company at a discount, thus shifting the risk of uncollectible debts that finance company). If you are selling small retail items or are in an industry where customers pay immediately your write-offs (also referred to as charge-offs or bad debts) will be low. However, if your typical sale is a high dollar amount you may want to run credit checks on potential customers before completing a sales contract committing you to spend money meeting the customer's needs.

Cash

After working hard through each pipe and bend in the sales pipeline you arrive at last with **cash** flowing out of the faucet. This seems like the end of the process, but I refer to this as a sales cycle because the end (cash) leads directly to the beginning (building marketplace awareness). It is not enough to clear clogs and patch leaks throughout the pipeline. If you receive several big orders and concentrate exclusively on fulfilling those contracts you will leave air bubbles in your sales pipeline. The result will be that cash coming out for a while may feel good, but when it stops you have to stuff as much time into the beginning of the pipeline and wade through all the time delays involved in navigating the entire pipeline before any cash flows again. Sometimes that can be a business life-threatening amount of time while expense obligations continue to drain you. So another part of your sales effort is to avoid air bubbles in the pipeline by devoting a full day or two every week towards prospecting for more customers, regardless of how many big orders you might temporarily have in hand to work on at the moment.

Priming the Pump

Also, don't forget that filling the pipeline includes taking some of the cash from sales to prime the prospecting pump again. The goal is to keep a full constant flow of sales effort throughout the entire sales cycle pipeline.

As a Christian business, there is an added moral obligation. Some struggling customers may need compassion and grace from time to time. If your product or service is not the highest quality (which happens in all businesses occasionally) our moral responsibility is to represent Christ's standards. This may involve taking a loss by replacing or repairing a product, or providing additional services at little to no cost. All of these issues must be factored into your pricing to create a sustainable gross profit margin and self-sustaining company or organization.

10

Strategies & Distribution Channels

Nearly everyone recognizes that it is more profitable to sell to a group of customers or convince other companies to sell your products or services than to invest the same amount of time selling just a single customer. Both are essential during the initial startup phase, but entire revenue streams will grow your company much faster than seeking customers one at a time, even though distribution channels usually take much longer to develop than bringing in a single customer. In this chapter, we will look more in-depth at the selling strategies mentioned earlier, as well as ideas for developing distribution channels.

Wholesale Distribution

A **distribution channel** is a path through which goods and services traverse to reach the end-user. For example, manufacturers traditionally seek to find several wholesalers or wholesaler chains that will market their products. In turn, wholesalers search for retailers within reasonable reach of their warehouses who will sell their products directly to end-users. An increasing number of manufacturers attempt to develop direct relationships with retailers, either via independent contractor salespeople, called manufacturing representatives, or by direct solicitation to retailers and retail chains.

Retail Customers

Some manufacturers set up their own **retailer customers** who sell to consumers. An example of this is car manufacturers who help set up and license dealerships. This allows the manufacturer to contractually require certain behaviors, such as purchasing a minimum number of cars per month, promoting their suggested manufacturer's retail price so the manufacturer's product line will not experience a perceived drop in value among consumers, and therefore tend to lower profit margins and possibly market share. To tie dealers closer to manufacturers, car manufacturers offer financing for inventory, and some will offer consignment terms. Selling on consignment amounts to the manufacturer delivering the product but waiting to get paid until their customer (the dealership) sells that inventory.

Making an end-run around one level of distribution channels is not limited to manufacturers. For example, Amazon is both a **wholesaler** and **retailer** of books and other items. Amazon purchases books in bulk to sell directly to consumers, thus bypassing retail outlets. It also acts as a commissioned sales platform for retailers selling to consumers by charging a fee for offering to online retailers a method of promoting goods and services to consumers, charging a storage and handling fee to smaller retailers for warehousing, and directly delivering the retailer's products to their consumers plus processing administrative chores such as collecting and paying the many hundreds of different sales taxes and the related monthly sales tax returns for small retailers.

Websites and Network Sales

Retailers likewise have sought to modify the traditional distribution channel structure by selling only via **websites** rather than more expensive "brick and mortar" storefront facilities, or by building a **network** of independent sales agents who work on straight commission, such as Alticor (the former Amway) and Mary Kay Cosmetics.

Franchise Models

Other entrepreneurs have found methods for building a network of stores without the need to pay for the high cost of opening retail stores in many locations. McDonald's is a great example. Ray Kroc initially tried to open multiple company-owned restaurants, but quickly recognized the huge limitation banks and other financing sources imposed upon him. Instead, he developed a **franchise model** to help each local licensed franchisee open and operate their own restaurants at their own cost while Kroc provided operations training, local and national advertising, and the pricing benefits of centralized bulk purchasing of products. The great insight of this franchise model to the franchisor is it brings in franchise fees instead of draining cash to open restaurants or storefronts.

Licensing

Perhaps the most innovative model for expanding a business very rapidly is the Coca-Cola model developed by entrepreneur Asa Candler. He kept the formula secret and carefully guarded it while licensing regional distributors (wholesalers) to license local bottling companies who sell to retail stores that sell to consumers.

Candler received **license revenue** from both the regional **distributors** (who earned fees from the local bottlers they signed up and sold to) plus from the local bottlers (whose license fees were split between the regional distributors and Candler's franchising company). With nearly no upfront expenses or cash drain on his company, Candler was free to spend a healthy portion of the fee revenue generated on advertising the brand name and auditing all licensed distributors to maintain quality control. Coca-Cola quickly became a massive cash machine with no significant manufacturing plants, regional offices, or any other expensive overhead for the primary company. Distributors were responsible for all of those hefty expenditures, and they had a big incentive to build the sales base for the primary company so their own local and regional franchises could thrive also.

Integrated Channel

A final model to consider is the **integrated channel**. A few manufacturers also set up company-owned wholesale companies and even retail outlets. Thus the manufacturer can control quality and profit margins with less regulatory expense by owning every step in the production-to-end-consumer chain. This approach tends to be the most costly in terms of the amount of cash needed, but some very innovative internet-based integrated channel models are growing at a hyper growth rate, which many accountants and economists define as annual growth in sales exceeding 40%. A recent example is the clothing manufacturer DSTLD.com which provides trendy young adult hipster fashion directly to consumers via its online retail store, and which is opening another regional wholesale warehouse to service customers on both coasts faster and more efficiently.

Choosing Your Distribution Channels

As you start your business one of the first decisions you should make after conducting your initial survey and discovering the types of people or businesses who are most likely to become your future customers is to consider how to reach the greatest number of them most frequently at the lowest cost to you. That is the first step towards developing a distribution channel (sometimes called a marketing or sales channel, especially for service businesses).

Choose one of the distribution channel paths already explained in this chapter. Start with a single channel to avoid spreading your efforts too thin. Attempt to discern the most direct link to potential customers, and do not expect channel partners to invest in promoting your product line. They are more interested in building their own sales and profits, so your company will need to spend money on advertising and conduct marketing efforts to supplement mere channel displays or offerings of your product line. This is where things like rebates and discount coupons can help.

Also consider how much support and incentive you might need to build into your distribution channels, such as offering floor financing (charging your distribution customers an interest cost for advancing products but letting them pay later), consignment terms, free marketing trips to resorts for top producers and other incentives.

Another important decision is defining for your industry and situation how many customers justify a distribution or advertising channel. Few startups have extra cash lying around to fund multiple distribution channels and marketing networks development initially. Plan on beginning with one distribution channel that you innervate and support to achieve strong results, rather than scattering scarce cash among multiple distribution channel development projects and probably achieving little to no sales results.

Creating Sales Synergy

When deciding on where to focus your channel development efforts for maximum result consider **up-selling** (selling more expensive or additional add-ons to your basic product or service offering), **cross-selling** (selling related or complementary products), and **partnering** (jointly encouraging sales of both your products and the selected products of other companies that fit well with your product line, thus creating synergy in total sales for both companies, such as software applications for hardware you sell).

Another selling approach is to either **bundle** a group of products or services to make an attractive package solving many customer needs. Conversely, you can offer **unbundling.** This can be strategic when your competitors are mostly bundling. This way, you can market your services as giving the customer more choice and lower cost from not being forced into buying features or services they do not want.

Selecting Your Strategy

Now let's move on from individual marketing and sales techniques to considering the bigger issue of strategy. Remember **Porter's Five Forces**? Which strategies have other companies found are most effective when one of these forces is a more dominant characteristic for your industry? The following chart should help you select a strategy most likely to help you succeed:

Porter's 5 Forces

		Strategies			
		Low-Cost Provider	Differentiation	Narrow Market Niche	Integrated
	Competition	No difference between your offering & competitors	Your product is distinct or you deliver faster	Find a niche the competition ignores or can't profitably service	Balance between price and features that attract
	Entry Ease	Costs cut low enough to undermine competitors' prices	Planned upgrades and new products to keep consumers interested	Niche is geographically or interest-wise difficult to spot & service	Temporary opportunity to grab quick market share, sell or merge
	Buyer Power	High, cuts profit forcing low-cost pricing. Low, should not be coupled with low-profit margins	Moderate to low fits this strategy allowing to make high-profit margins on unique features	Too narrow a niche gives high bargaining power. Target a size-able segment to weaken buyer power	The weaker the power the better integrated the strategy. High buyer power → transition to low-cost provider approach
	Seller Power	High seller power + low-cost provider sales = out of business	In a high seller power footing, the unique differentiated offerings must be priced with high margins	Affluent narrow niche markets work well in a high seller power exigency by offering profit margins	Mid-range pricing works if competitors are limited by high seller power or if buyer and seller's power are weak
	Substitution Threat	A highly restricted market can work with low-profit margins. Easy substitutes lead low-cost providers into bankruptcy	If substitution threats are high the differentiation strategy requires constant improvements to keep new entrants at bay	If customers can easily switch to substitutes then you must build a new niche or customize products rapidly	Integrated pricing and product strategy can hold on to market share for a substantial amount of time

Pipeline Metrics

After selecting the marketing and sales strategy that you think will maximize your probability of success, it is important to develop appropriate **metrics** for monitoring progress so you can make changes swiftly when essential. Think about the sales cycle pipeline. Each step in the pipeline and each possible area for clogs and leakage should have a metric for monitoring the flow of effort towards collecting sales cash. The beginning of the sales cycle is the most difficult to develop appropriate monitors for, but it is still possible.

Listed below are some possible metrics to consider. This is not a complete inventory of small business sales statistics by any stretch of the imagination! And you may feel not all of these metrics are appropriate or worth the time and cost to track, but they should give you a good starting point.

Pipeline Phase to Monitor	Suggested Metrics
Market Place Awareness	<ul><li>The number of inquiries and sources.</li><li>The number of sales calls or visits per day or week.</li><li>Length of time between follow-up contacts.</li></ul>
Delays Closing Sales	<ul><li>Longer-term trend tracking of sales volume sorted by key broad factors.</li><li>Number and description of most common prospect objections.</li></ul>

Sales	- Dollar volume: monthly totals and average sale per order. - Cost per order. - The number of visits, contacts, calls, and other communication per new customer. - Demographics: new versus repeat customers, number of repeat orders year-to-date, sales by niche identifications, etc. - Volume and dollar value of referrals.
Unrealistic Expectations or Promises	- Promised delivery date versus actual. - The number of times promised delivery was delayed. - Discounts from standard company pricing—frequency and percentages. - Number and nature of change orders.

WIP	• Dollar-cost and average time in each stage of production. • Dollar variance of actual vs. budgeted cost and production time per order. • Recurrence of notifications from production staff to sales staff of any delays or change in pricing needed.
Write-downs	• Volume and cost of reductions in sales orders. • Categorization of write-down reasons.
Accounts Receivable	• Dollar amount billed, sorted by 30-day aged periods. • Receivables sorted by a salesperson. • Turnover of receivables sorted by a salesperson. • The average percent of period and year-to-date sales tied up in receivables.

Write-offs	- The dollar cost of write-offs sorted by reason code: early payment discount, customer quality complaint, customer financial problem, etc. - Write-offs (dollar and percent of sales) sorted by a salesperson. - Cost to collect slow or no pay accounts.
Cash Collections	- Dollar volume sorted by product/service, salesperson, geographic area, type of advertising, or any other criteria that help you determine which are the most productive sales sources. - Accounts receivable turnover ratio. - Inventory turnover.

Don't worry about how you will gather the information for these metrics. We will discuss small business software packages that pull these types of statistics together for you later in the book.

The Bigger Picture

All of these metrics, strategy considerations, and pricing approaches are important, but keep your eye on the bigger picture these facets of your business are telling you about. The ultimate decision you, the entrepreneur, must make is whether to firmly commit to your vision and persevere against all the startup challenges, or pivot one or more aspects of your original business model to swiftly respond to data that may be giving you early warning signs about potential customers not accepting your original vision on what you think people will buy. This is a tough judgment call, and there is no set statistic to tell you when to hold on or when to change direction. Potential and existing customers' reactions found in these metrics give you clues about what changes are necessary and when. We will cover this later in more detail.

Let me make one final comment concerning marketing and sales strategies and distribution channels. As Christian business owners, we represent Christ in the marketplace. As such our ethical behavior should be solidly grounded in Biblical ideas and direction, and our focus should be on serving our customers, meeting their needs. If you concentrate on that approach, you will not have to watch your bottom line profit closely. Grateful customers will sense your concern for them, and many will in effect help watch your profitability for you via referrals, positive comments to other consumers and business owners, not making unreasonable demands, and similar ways to help you grow your business.

Not every customer will be grateful, but many will sense and be attracted to this Biblical mindset of conducting business. For those customers who are not grateful (the 20% of the old 80/20 Rule that says the top 20% of customers provide most of your profit at the least effort and expense while the bottom 20% tend to be the most costly and troublesome) I look upon them as "potential future Christians. " I might need to "fire" unprofitable customers if they create too much disruption. But I should always make the effort to display a higher ethical way to conduct business and seek opportunities to witness to them about Jesus.

III

Operations

This section covers operation approaches from developing systems-based efforts to efficiently organizing your production efforts.

Chapter 11 explores methods of efficiency through systems thinking.

Chapter 12 explores methods of efficiency through lean operations.

Chapter 13 provides theories for setting up and managing your buyer actions.

Chapter 14 discusses the pros and cons of automation & outsourcing.

11

Systems Thinking

Your operations should be as effective and efficient as possible to assure consistent, profitable delivery of products and services to customers. This chapter focuses on the first part—effectiveness. Consider the types of activities you repeat within your business to provide effective results. In an earlier chapter, we discussed the marketing and sales cycle. The operations or production cycle is another aspect of delivering consistent quality results. As your business grows you may want to diagram other cycles of activity within your company as a helpful way to identify inefficiencies and ineffective activities ripe for improvement.

Cycles

What exactly is a cycle? Simply put, a **cycle** is a series of activities that must be repeated endlessly for the business to survive and prosper. As soon as you complete a sale the company must be prepared to deliver the product or service sold in a manner that delights the customer yet at a cost that earns the company a profit. Synergistically organizing your delivery method is the heart of the systems thinking theory.

Each step in a process leads to the next, and this interconnectedness can either speed or delay your ability to fulfill the sales obligations you pursued. As you design your initial production system and modify it when the company grows, the regular review of each step of employee action, paperwork, and expenditure timing helps you see opportunities to improve both effectiveness and efficiency. The goal is to keep production moving swiftly, with high-quality output and as minimal waste as possible.

To illustrate the **systems thinking** concept, pretend you own a retail ice cream shop in a typical strip mall. The operations cycle begins with estimating the volume and flavors of ice cream and other supplies (cones, scoopers, freezers, display boards, etc.) you will need over the next month, how much inventory is on hand now, a reasonable minimum level of inventory to maintain by month end to sell into early next month, and the timing of how long it usually takes from date of placing an order to when your vendor's truck pulls up with the delivery. The most efficient way to assure you always have enough products to sell but do not tie up too much money in excessively high inventory levels would be to develop a spreadsheet where you can input these figures, costs, and dates every month.

Illustration

Next, think through the physical layout of the store. It should channel customers to one end where they look at all the attractive ice cream flavors properly labeled so customers can make their selections early in the process. Moving down the line you could have various toppings displayed as well as various types of cones or container sizes offered. At the following station, your employees could offer additional products such as drinks, napkins, utensils, or candy bars. In another area, your employees could ask whether the customer intends to eat the ice cream at your shop or take it elsewhere. The customer's response would determine whether you place the products in travel containers or not. Finally, the customer's last transaction stop should be where he or she pays for the products. If the customer plans to eat the ice cream in your store the last place the customer would move to is a chair and table.

An additional aspect of your operating cycle would be the scheduling of employees to assure that you are fully staffed to minimize wait queues for customers while not wasting cash paying for too many employees to stand around waiting for customers to enter. Another spreadsheet or payroll program can help you with employee scheduling. You might also have a sign-in sheet to keep track of when employees come and go, and perhaps to let them leave notes requesting time off or changes in shifts.

Efficiency Improvements

As your business continues to grow it would be prudent to consider other efficiency improvements. For example, nearly all modern cash registers produce a **Z tape** which lists each transaction for the day or shift (depending on how you program it) as well as totals for the number of transactions, types of products sold, cash sales, credit card sales and any other data you want to track.

Comparing the Z tape after each shift while counting cash in the register at the end of each shift (and depositing any amounts above the minimum you need to make change for customers) will tell you if your cash register employee is making math errors when providing change or (hopefully not) stealing, and which employee is responsible for managing the register for that shift.

Likewise, using an **inventory sheet** to count your inventory periodically helps you determine how much inventory is stolen, wasted, melted, or otherwise unaccounted for. You will need to start with the amount on hand at the beginning of the count date, add ice cream (or other products) for each flavor added to the display cases (or loaded off vendor trucks into your big "back office" freezer), minus the amount your Z tape says you sold, to arrive at what the ending inventory should be—versus the actual amount you count.

Remember our discussion on triple loop learning? As your hypothetical ice cream shop grows we need to apply triple loop learning to re-define quality and output capacity, especially for the service portion of our little ice cream store. The goal is to seek innovative changes in products, operations, and growth flexibility. A secondary objective is to strengthen internal control to prevent theft and waste without inhibiting operations.

For example, we might purchase a simple time clock device mounted on the wall to more accurately and conveniently track each employee's shift check-in and out times. The clock device can be linked wirelessly to the computer's accounting and payroll software. To improve operational flow substantially, we could mount ice cream dispensers on a wall and include a "salad bar" type of self-serve display case for toppings and other accouterments.

This shop layout redesign would speed the product delivery for customers. Employees would now collect customer payment at the beginning of the line and hand them a cone or container. Customers could choose their ice cream flavors and toppings. Drinks could be sold from wall dispensers as well. Installing low-cost, wireless sensors on the ice cream and drink tanks could alert the employee at the cash register when supplies of products are getting low enough to trigger a refill warning, eliminating the possibility of a negative customer experience due to the unavailability of products.

To accommodate a greater number of customers you could also add weather-proof tables and chairs outside the shop. In certain climates, the shop might even have outside rockers to add more character and enjoyment to the customer experience. Not only would customers receive faster service, but you would also save on the reduced number of employees needed to fully cover each shift.

Triple loop learning includes reviewing the cycles for sales and delivery to find additional methods for improving service. For example, you might offer a small financial incentive or bonus to employees for cost savings, increased marketing, and sales ideas, or operational improvements that enhance customers' service experience.

Employees might suggest utilizing social media tools or developing a phone application so customers could order and pay for products before they arrive at the store, and receive a modest volume discount for purchasing a large volume of orders simultaneously or perhaps for a certain volume of loyalty purchases over a specified period, or for referring friends who link to the original customer's app account when ordering. The employee would take only a few seconds to scan the barcode or pull up the confirmation transaction on a company computer to confirm the purchase has already been paid for, then hand the cone or container products, prepared when the order was put in the company's electronic order cue. Social media marketing and the phone app could also be set to offer discounts or publicity such as a free tee-shirt after enough purchases to both incentivize customers and publicize your store.

Note that using social media, product reorder sensors and other low-cost technology also automates inventory tracking and sales tracking while minimizing the number of cash transactions, and therefore increasing internal controls against theft, waste, and spoilage. Encouraging employees to consider how each step in the operations cycle might be shortened or paperwork eliminated leads to continual incremental improvements that, over time, result in substantially greater customer satisfaction and sales volume while boosting the profits of the business. We will discuss employee and vendor development in a later chapter, but for now, consider how operational effectiveness can be constantly improved.

Also, consider how a change in one area affects other parts of the operation, and therefore the synergy of the entire organization. Pondering changes in your operations becomes more important as your company continues to grow, so it stays flexible enough to swiftly respond to market changes. The systems approach considers how a change in one step may affect others, with the goal of creating synergy across the entire organization. Therefore, your objective should be to understand the dynamics, constraints, and the overall environment within which the system of operations functions.

Reducing variability should be a major goal. If you design your operating system to be robust then both quality and quantity should remain steady, minimizing wasted time and resources. Yet the objective is not 100% avoidance of all variability, since your operations must retain enough flexibility to respond quickly to unique situations and changes in the marketplace. Also, recognize no system will work indefinitely in a constantly changing environment without frequent fine-tuning and the occasional major overhaul.

Illustration

Consider the example of a small manufacturing company producing small engines and replacement parts for small engine repair shops. The traditional approach to improving product offerings was to spend months drawing specifications for new parts, then spending thousands of dollars on producing a prototype part which was then tested apart from the assembly line on an older unit. This trial and error method almost always required multiple repetitions of this design and testing cycle, since the new test part might not perform as expected or a machine failure might be due to using an older engine in which a worn-out part rather than the new test part failed.

A more efficient method might be to utilize CAD/CAM computer engineering design software, which has become very affordable, to develop part and engine objectives and test parameters under a variety of virtual conditions. Parts could be virtually designed, and after testing within the software a low-cost 3D printer could print the test part cheaply for inclusion in a new model engine. The entire research and the testing cycle could be reduced by months or years (depending upon which industry you manufacture for) and save many thousands of dollars. If your company uses a computerized assembly line the new part can be implemented into the manufacturing process very quickly. Do not forget that no matter how high-tech or philosophical your modeling aspires to be, there is no replacement for good old-fashioned common sense from both you and your employees when developing good operational systems.

Measuring

Highly effective operational systems require regular measuring to provide you with feedback when any portion of your operations begins to degrade. How should an entrepreneur design a measurement and reporting system? Start at the desired end or output and work backward to the beginning point of the operational systems cycle. This approach often helps identify unnecessary steps or paperwork.

Consider what is important at each step. For example, for an online wholesale business, it is important to track not only whether you receive all the product ordered, but also the amount that is spoiled, broken, or otherwise unsaleable plus the amount of time the product is in the warehouse before shipping to a retail customer. As the operation grows you might add another means of tracking, such as the time delay between ordering product to when it is disgorged on your loading dock, how long it takes your employees to enter it into your inventory system, and load it only the appropriate warehouse shelf, and the time delay between receiving payment for online orders versus the actual shipping date of the product.

Depending on your particular industry and product or service mix other measurements can be developed. The key to designing a good internal control system is thinking through all the clogs and leaks that might occur in your system. Be aware that just because you can design a monitor or statistic does not mean you should! Consider the cost versus the benefit, leaving some flexibility and trust in your employees to produce efficiently and effectively without feeling over-monitored, which can lower their morale and effectiveness.

Final Thoughts

Let me add one final thought on systems thinking: Designing what you believe is an effective operations system and measuring key performance steps or actions along that system does not tell you whether the performance is great, modest, poor, or otherwise. What is the best reference point to measure against? You might set your targets, but how do you know your personal judgment is the most effective approach?

One approach is to set employees competing against each other or make changes in their working environment. For example, the famous steel magnate Andrew Carnegie decided one day to ask one of his production teams how many ingots they produced during their shift. He then wrote that number down on the floor in large font with chalk and left. When Carnegie returned a week later the number had been erased and replaced with a new number nearly double as high. What had happened is the next shift asked why the number was written on the floor. Soon every crew in every shift felt the need to prove they were the best, creating a huge boost in productivity at no additional cost to Carnegie.

Another approach to motivating employees was an experiment Westinghouse conducted at its Hawthorne plant in Cicero, Illinois. Managers periodically changed something in the work environment, whether the intensity of overhead lighting or temperature within the plant, or some other environmental or routine aspect of factory work. Each time a change occurred there was some increase in productivity, even if the change was made back to the original conditions.

Perhaps a better standard to measure against is either internal benchmarks based on your company's trends over six months or greater or based on comparing various activities against the "best practices" performance published by consultants to your industry. There are various publishers, trade associations, and websites that provide benchmarking data for you to utilize as a reference for measuring how well each part of your business system is performing.

While developing your operational cycle and setting both measurements and benchmarks, it may be difficult to create such measurements for your efforts to share Jesus in your company and the marketplace. Later in this book, we will explain measurements others are using. For now, simply consider how you might incorporate measurements that reflect the inherent flexibility or variability in such efforts and avoidance of any legalistic type of numbers emphasis that undermines the person-to-person natural exchange of ideas, and personal concern the Bible calls us to express towards others.

12

Lean Operations

Effectiveness and Efficiency

Effectiveness focuses on issues including maintaining quality, and satisfying customer needs. **Efficiency** concentrates on getting the job done at the lowest possible cost and as quickly as practical while maintaining high quality. Both are important to satisfy customers.

Efficiency is typically associated with reducing waste and cost and speedy throughput. A truly lean operation includes all of these, recognizing some trade-offs may be acceptable rather than attempting the impossible to maximize every one of these factors. The **lean operations** principle can be applied to every area of your business operations.

However, as a Christian entrepreneur, it is important to take the time to listen to employees, vendors, customers, and others. Your main opportunity to share the Gospel in the marketplace will arise in one-on-one conversations, usually in trusting relationships built over time. The lean operations concept can undermine those sharing opportunities. Each entrepreneur must decide where they will draw the line between operational effectiveness and allowing personal relationships to spread community and foster Biblical ideas.

Lean Operations

With that balancing intention in mind, consider areas where you can build **lean operations**. Most people quickly think about scheduling meetings and appointments, using email, chat services, and other electronic tools for organization, and minimizing unproductive time. Likewise, the layout of your shop or office can affect efficiency.

There are additional areas, though, for creating lean operations that are important to consider. For example, in addition to minimizing the cost of products and overhead expenses, you could tighten cash flow. This is particularly important for product-oriented businesses (especially seasonal ones) that need bank lines of credit to fund product or parts purchases.

One popular lean operational approach to cash flow involves speeding up sales collections while arranging for slower payment of bills owed. If the product is an expensive one, many businesses ask for a downpayment.

Just In Time

Suppose you have buyer power with your suppliers, in other words, you purchase a volume of products that is significant to your vendor's sales, typically over five percent of their sales. In that case, you can arrange for Just In Time (JIT) inventory delivery.

The JIT concept involves an arrangement between you and your key suppliers to buy all or the majority of certain parts or products from them. In exchange, the supplier agrees to have a minimum amount of inventory on hand to deliver to you within 24 hours on-demand.

This allows you to collect cash from your customer, then order the inventory (rather than tying up your cash with products on the shelf) and deliver quickly to your customer, hopefully collecting the balance upon product delivery. Thus you are paying your supplier with your customer's cash rather than your own company cash. For some industries, you can nearly eliminate the need for bank borrowing and the related interest expense.

To improve overall customer satisfaction, lean activities will allow for the elimination of unwanted product features that use resources such as time or money but do not add value for the customer. Returning to our ice cream shop example, reorganizing operational flow—so that the customer pays first then dispenses the ice cream and toppings themselves—provides two benefits. First, the amount of time waiting to be served is greatly reduced. Second, by saving employee labor costs, you can share some of the savings with both employees and customers while increasing your margin. Customers appreciate a price break, and passing on some of the savings to employees, if done correctly, will motivate employees to make the customer purchasing experience more enjoyable.

Kanban

There are several well-established methods for improving efficiency. Perhaps the most simple is called Kanban. Toyota industrial engineer Talichi Ohno developed this method. Cards, or more commonly bar code scanning,[13] mark the time spent in each of the stages in the assembly line. One can easily follow the work-in-process components through the operations system.[14]

This approach requires setting an upper limit for the number of components waiting at the beginning or end of a process to prevent clogs of excessive work in progress. The cards represent requests for raw materials or input to the current manufacturing stage and notification for replenishment at each production stage. In other words, the cards are a simple, low-tech method for tracking reorder levels and minimizing disruptions to the steady flow of production.

---

[13] Scan the barcode stamped on a key part in an assembly line.

[14] Staging, preparation, actual improvement modification (production), and wait time to ship to the next station.

Kaizen

Another lean operations approach that includes a triple loop learning dimension is Kaizen events.[15] This concept involves halting production in a plant or office for one day while the management and staff walk through each step of the daily operations. They carefully document and discuss the labor required as well as the input, output, and scrap result in order to identify and eliminate any unnecessary labor, paperwork, and movements. The goal is to identify and eliminate unnecessary labor, paperwork, and movements.

The Hedgehog Concept

Another idea often classified as a lean operational concept, but which could just as easily be considered a core competency notion, is the Hedgehog Concept first noted by researcher Jim Collins. Like the boring but stubbornly determined animal, the Hedgehog Concept quite simply notes that the most successful companies identified one thing they perform best, and then tenaciously pursued perfection in both production of and speed in that one thing. The corporations which used the Hedgehog Concept rocketed to the top of their industries. However, they had to spend many years understanding and building the execution of that one best action.

Professor Collins describes this effort as akin to a hamster beginning to run on a wheel. Over time the wheel moves

---

[15] It was developed in Japan from the advice of American management consultant Peter Drucker.

ever faster as momentum builds. All other "second best things" are outsourced or discarded. Meanwhile, the company focuses on constant improvement of the action to become the very best amongst their peers. In conjunction with this idea, Dr. Collins points out that top-performing companies seek both employees and operational improvements that lie at the intersection of three objectives:

1. What you are most passionate about.
2. What you can be the best in the world at performing.
3. What best drives your economic or resource engine.

If any employee or company operational cycle fails at achieving results in the intersection of these three objectives, then that employee or operational effort should be terminated or outsourced to a vendor specializing in that function.

Triple Loop Learning Theory

There are other lean operational concepts. These often incorporate **triple loop learning theory**. You may be familiar with triple-loop learning theory, even if you think you aren't. For example, General Electric's former Chief Executive Officer Jack Welch implemented a form of the theory, developed by Motorola engineer Bill Smith, called **Lean Six Sigma**.

This is a customer-focused strategy for constant improvement at a minimal or lean expense. The "Lean" portion of the title refers to the part of the goal specified in terms of lowest cost or quickest completion of the operational step, while simultaneously achieving near-zero defects or waste. The "six" refers to six standard deviations between the process mean and the nearest error-free goal or maximum possible quality result (referred to by the Greek letter Sigma). The intent is to move the mean as close to perfection as possible in quality.

Yet another theory that covers both effectiveness and efficiency is **Total Quality Management (TQM)**. Its aim is to achieve maximum customer satisfaction through a continual process. This process involves detecting and reducing or eliminating errors in manufacturing, distribution, and all other aspects of the customer experience. How the TQM goals are defined by management makes a difference in whether this approach always results in the lowest cost (even at some reduced customer satisfaction) or improved customer satisfaction at a higher cost. Either way, management defines efficiency in terms of customer service after surveying customers for what they value in the purchasing and support services aspects.

Queuing Theory

For some services, efficiency might not be defined as maximizing customer delight if that is not a usual expectation for the industry. Consider banking as an example. If you walk into a physical bank branch, you expect to wait in line to see the teller or bank officer. For an industry such as banking, efficiency might be considered an optimum wait time that minimizes the cost of bank employee costs while not creating such a long wait that it irritates customers. This type of mathematical modeling is called **Queuing Theory**. One prominent type of queuing theory is **Little's Law**. Invented by Professor John Little in 1961 at the Massachusetts Institute of Technology (MIT), the formula is stated as follows:

$$L = \lambda W$$

In a stationary or **stable system**[16] or, in other words, when customers enter at a constant rate, the number of customers (L) willing to wait an extended time (W) will eventually drop to an equilibrium level of lower sales (λ).

Hopefully, this has helped you see the variety of ways you can apply a lean operational effort. For review and future exploration, here are key areas to eliminate various types of waste or inefficiency:

1. Worker jobs
2. Inventory management
3. Transportation
4. Facilities and operational layout
5. Decision-making such as cutting unnecessary meetings or requiring specified advanced preparation including uploaded PowerPoint slides that reduce the length of the meeting
6. Cash flow administration

Let me add a huge word of caution. One area NOT to cut is marketing and sales. Entrepreneurs tend to reduce expendi-

---

[16] This is not true in many queuing situations because they have peak and trough times.

tures in this area first, but nothing else in your operation will be sustained if the company cannot first bring in cash from sales.

The famous department store entrepreneur John Wanamaker—the man credited with creating the advertising industry—was once asked by fellow Philadelphia merchants if he recognized that much of his advertising expense was wasted. His cheerful response was that he always assumed half of what he spent on advertising was wasted. "The trouble is," he said, "I don't know which half."

However, like anything else, marketing and advertising should have budget constraints. For established companies, marketing and advertising expenses are typically a percentage of sales, earmarked to be reinvested in gaining more business. However, it is difficult to determine with accuracy what is simultaneously a lean promotional budget and an effective sales lead generator. People are endlessly frustrating when it comes to targeted marketing. They do not always respond as predicted (according to the sales team's or accounting department's predictors). And when they do respond, it may take a significant amount, energy, and budget of time to convert a sales lead into a paying customer.

For example, in my CPA practice, I saw some prospects take up to two years to become clients, while others responded swiftly. This disparity makes accurate tracking of responses challenging. That is also why I suggest following the pipeline analogy. Some prospect "water" in the pipeline moves faster than others. The key is to avoid "air bubbles" (no potential sales you are currently working on). Tie system metrics to components that keep the prospect/sales flow moving.

In summary, look at your lean operations attempts as an internal consultant role:

1. attempting to analyze other possible ways to perform the required action,
2. then evaluate which brainstorming approach might yield the most effective and efficient results.

To try out some of these methods, subsystems can be tested as well as an overall operational system. The idea is to magnify the subsystem to the size of the overall system in order to provide clarity. Subsystems can be a smaller component of a larger operation. Or they can be differing efforts required for segmented customer types by the level of services, types of products, or other delineation.

When you implement a change, test that change by seeking feedback from employees, customers, and possibly suppliers. Begin with celebrating small improvements and changing incentives so old, undesirable behavior is not rewarded, and new, desirable behavior is encouraged.

Allow some risk-taking by employees and reward that behavior publicly. Entrepreneurial organizations tend to be better at allowing risk-taking than larger, more structured, or bureaucratic companies, but much depends upon your confidence in your employees' mature judgment. If, after sufficient time to adjust to the modification, the results of the new operational procedure are still the same or worse, focus on identifying the bottlenecks. Analyze whether speedier throughput is possible by returning to the older method. It may happen that some other aspect of your operational cycle also needs to be improved.

While we have noted that it can be possible for the individual employees to need to be cut in a lean operating model, remember: Always treat your employees with kindness in this process. It may take time and energy to discover if they are indeed incapable of adjusting to a new system or modifying undesirable behavior. However, no matter what, display the virtue of Christian kindness. It may be necessary to be firm in your decisions, but don't be hasty, rude, or dismissive.

13

Supply Chain Management

Whether you are selling products or services, your supply chain is vital to the growth and sustainability of your company. A good definition of **supply chain** is a system of organizations, people, activities, resources, and possibly information involved in moving a product or service from supplier to customer. During the supply chain movement, raw materials develop into a final product or a delivered service. This chapter covers the theories most helpful to smaller startup enterprises for developing and managing buyer actions.

If you are selling products, your supply chain most likely includes the following steps in the order listed:

1. Purchase raw materials (or products to fill your shelves)
2. Inbound transport arrangements
3. Partial or complete assembly of parts — if a manufacturer. Storage at a warehouse or at a contracted company — if a wholesaler or retailer
4. Quality control checks (both interim and final)

5. Outbound transport arrangements
6. Deliver finished goods to customers

If you are a service business there are still supply chain elements. They typically are:

1. Interview and hire—if an employee. Contract—if an independent subcontractor or a firm—on either ongoing or contract-by-contract basis, setting parameters of what work they will do versus what you will perform and what client contact level is permissible.
2. Schedule workdays, location, and completion date.
3. Review secure control over any client data obtained and quality check the final report, whether presented orally or written.
4. Follow up with the client for additional questions and comments on the quality of service.

If you started a nonprofit organization, the products or services steps in your supply chain will probably involve additional steps. Namely, *Training and managing volunteers in two different capacities:*

- Delivery of products or services to end-users. Most charities refer to these people as "clients" even though they are not paying full price or often nothing
- Donor support, including both cash and non-cash tangible gifts plus volunteer time and talents

Blended Employee and Vendor Startups

Either employees or vendors might perform each step. Startup organizations are not simply smaller versions of bigger companies. There are unique aspects to startup companies before they morph into larger mature companies. Picture it as being similar to the tadpole, which has quite different abilities, required environmental conditions, and appearance from its later stage mature frog. Eventually, your company will mature into the typical larger operation, but initially, the line between employee and vendor is often blurred. Many startup companies are forced by limited capital to outsource most of the company's operational cycle to outside vendors. To provide high quality to customers, interview vendors for understanding and motivation to help you deliver your product or service as well as reliability and consistent, high-quality performance.

A small real estate business is a typical example of a blended employee and vendor startup, as well as a transition into the more traditional established model. The firm's owner is the registered broker, and all sales associates (realtors) are almost always considered independent contractors. As a startup, small real estate firms might contract with the local Multiple Listing Service (MLS) and also allow their sales agents to upload property listings to a company website.

Allocate most of the money from your initial limited capital to brand awareness and promotional efforts. Some real estate entrepreneurs contract with a call center in a low-cost nation, such as the Philippines, or perhaps forward calls to a homemaker who contracts to be the firm's answering service to receive potential customers' calls and allocate among sales associates.

As cash flow improves, the owner seeks to replace the outsourced call center vendor with an employee in the office. With continued improvement, the owner could rent additional space for a conference room and perhaps a couple of work cubicles. However, many independent realtors prefer to work from their home laptops and cell phones or meet customers in their cars. Real estate firms no longer need a large amount of startup capital to rent a large office and hire a receptionist immediately due to the ability to leverage technology to keep initial costs low.

What does this look like in practice? A good case example is a pharmaceutical company. Several years ago, one of my clients started an online over-the-counter pharmacy selling non-prescription products. As a startup, he built a website using standard, low-cost shopping cart software integrated into his website and linked to the bank merchant account he contracted with for collecting bank drafts and plastic cards (both debit and credit). The supplier he located for his initial set of products was based in Poland and willing to dropship anywhere in the world for advance payment. In case you are unfamiliar with the term, "dropship" means your vendor will send the product directly to your customer without any need for you to hold it as inventory in a warehouse you rent directly.

My client set up his company website to provide autoresponders to both the customer confirming the sale and another to the vendor in Poland. The vendor's message included delivery instructions, the quantity of product, and a wire transaction number from the merchant banking software that sent an agreed-upon amount per-product unit for each sale collected. This left my client free to focus on advertising efforts, responding to prospects, customer emails, chat boxes, and visiting the Polish manufacturer periodically. During his visits, he checked product quality, controlled sampling, and complied with the legal agreement requiring underground storage and regular purge of customer identification data.

As the company grew rapidly, the entrepreneur had to hire additional employees to respond to inquiries and eventually to assure customer data was kept secure, especially after adding more suppliers and product lines. He set up contracted warehouse arrangements in several locations which printed automated labels for warehouse staff to stick onto packages sent from Poland and other suppliers. Still, the customer data was stored under his sole control at the company website hosting service and a backup site. Assuming the company continues to grow rapidly the entrepreneur will gradually bring more of these supply chain steps internally, although probably not all.

The key to building a consistent, high-quality product or service startup company is setting up your supply chain as interlinked networks between vendors, employees, and sometimes customers. This concept applies to all types of companies, from manufacturers and wholesalers to retailers, both product and service companies. The chain must function smoothly. If you cannot find or if you outgrow a vendor, that is a signal it might be time to bring that particular function in-house using employees rather than outside contractors.

Partnering

At the same time, be careful how much integration you allow between your company and your vendors. A popular Silicon Valley term for limited sharing of ideas and companies working together on projects is the word "**partnering**." This idea intentionally falls far short of the Japanese Keiretsu or South Korean Zaibatzu arrangements. In Japan and South Korea, the supply chain is legally fully integrated. While each company usually has "independent" majority ownership, each link in the supply chain[17] are shareholders in each other's companies.

This Asian arrangement allows employees and vendors to meet frequently and discuss product development, delivery timing, profit margins, and other topics that are considered a violation of antitrust laws in the United States and nearly all Western nations. Thus, although it is sometimes possible for vendors to work alongside company employees, for American companies, it is an antitrust violation and illegal in most cases.

---

[17] Manufacturer of parts, wholesalers, service firms, retail outlets, banks lending to all of the above, and a government agency such as the Ministry of Trade and Industry.

So some integration can help build your startup company, but too much can cause you serious legal ramifications.

Logistics

Much of what is described in this chapter involves **logistics**. The term logistics means the transport and storage portion of the supply chain. Logistical issues cause the majority of the "**bullwhip effect**," which is a result of shortages and overproduction, similar to stop-and-go traffic jams. The root cause of this problem is miss-information conveyed up and down the supply chain, causing inaccurate demand forecasting and ordering, thus wasting resources and causing potential customer dissatisfaction. The lesson to learn from this challenge is to build an adequate and frequent communication system alongside each physical shipment to keep the proper flow of product or service throughout the supply chain operation.

Take note that the supply chain involves products or services sold to customers. While important, support functions[18] are not part of the supply chain management, which concentrates upon production for satisfying customer demands. In order to apply Dr. Collins's idea of concentrating on your company providing the best service to customers, at the beginning you should outsource all support functions. Pay for them piecemeal as needed until you are large enough to justify the

---

[18] Accounting, legal, marketing, sales, financing, executive leadership, human resource management, etc.

steady overhead cost of internal, employer-supplied support services.

14

Automation & Outsourcing

Technological advances have created many opportunities to cut overhead costs through the use of computers and robots and outsourcing peripheral tasks to other companies—especially lower-cost firms in developing nations. However, always keep in mind how customers perceive these actions. It is unproductive for your business growth to save a few dollars and some time at the expense of many thousands in lost sales due to customer perception.

Customer Interaction

Although it remains beneficial to automate and outsource some activities, any operation that affects customer interaction with your business should be carefully handled. Customer relations is an area where smaller companies can often outshine their larger competitors.

An obvious starting point is any administrative or internal support function that does not affect customer relations. Examples include cloud-based accounting, payroll services, HR services if you offer employee benefit plans, fleet tracking if your company operates a fleet of trucks or cars and similar support services. Inventory reordering levels and factory assembly operations can also benefit from robotic and computer applications. Beyond administrative and basic production activities, consider the impact on customer perception of your company.

For example, your website can utilize autoresponder emails to provide quick acknowledgment to prospects. Some outsourced call center functions can still give customers a great feeling about your company while you avoid the high cost of full-time customer support personnel. Certain nations, such as the Philippines and Ireland, work well for employee and customer message taking. I have also seen some of my clients contract with farm wives in rural areas of the United States to provide friendly, fully English, yet more affordable call support.

An increasing number of companies are beginning to apply robots and other automation solutions to replace outsourcing firms. By now you have most likely experienced robotic voice recognition services for call-in customer support or voice recognition services such as Amazon's Alexa. Robots and artificial intelligence will continue to replace "blue-collar" factory jobs. Offshore firms and artificial intelligence will replace "white-collar" jobs in areas such as government compliance functions and basic diagnostic services as well.

In areas where an aging population is creating a growing labor shortage, this trend will accelerate, which will make your use of such technology increasingly more acceptable to prospects and customers. For example, in some Tokyo restaurants, the only human I met was the maitre d' upfront, and the restaurant had a cook in the back who monitored several artificial intelligence devices that automated much of the actual cooking. We ordered from a device on the table (which is already becoming more common in the United States) and a little robot delivered the food tray to our table.

How much can be outsourced or automated? The limit is set by your creativity and whether customers might respond negatively to any change. For internet-based companies, customers have already become accustomed to a lack of direct phone support or live chat, and fully automated search, selection, and payment options. That does not mean customers are happy with this situation.

Depending on your marketing strategy, this could fit well with a company goal to be a low-cost provider, but adding personal support would probably increase sales for a company with a differentiation or "status" strategy (luxury goods, cutting edge technology product offerings, or building brand desirability).

The key entrepreneurial component so prevalent in America is creativity—a large disadvantage for more collectivist cultures, which by their nature struggle with producing innovation. How should Christian entrepreneurs respond to workers in each type of environment? If you utilize offshore contractors, then study their home culture to design compensation and tasks that motivate them and aim to their strengths. Can your offshore vendor handle exceptions and unusual customer situations? If not, those transactions or functions should remain within your company, performed by your employees.

While poor vendor English skills and lack of understanding about the American marketplace can hurt your sales and company image, automation has even less flexibility and frequently generates customer irritation over cumbersome phone routing systems or extensive website routing methodology that offers no human interaction. If you decide to pursue much outsourcing or automation, then also include automated customer surveys combined with some random human direct call surveys, so you can keep a pulse on how customers feel about these operational approaches. In addition, while automation can save you money, sometimes retooling an automated assembly line or reprogramming computer or website functions can be more expensive than outsourcing.

Remember, managing these stakeholder relationships with vendors can be tricky from a regulatory viewpoint, as well as cultural considerations. Review the IRS web page entitled "Independent Contractor (Self-Employed) or Employee?" and download IRS form SS-8, which is the checklist IRS agents use to reclassify subcontractors for purposes of assessing additional employee payroll taxes. The SS-8 form lists the areas that distinguish contractor versus employee. In summary, an employee is someone you have control over, directing the employee what hours to work, where, which tasks to perform, deadlines to meet, and other supervisory actions you can command. You do not have control over any of these things with a true contractor, who also has multiple customers besides you and the vendor's own office space.

Customers will hold you accountable for performance by your vendors and automated systems as well as for how well your employees meet customer expectations. Consider whether customers are best served with multiple options. For example, Intuit (provider of TurboTax) offers several versions of "do it yourself" tax return preparation software for various prices, plus an add-on option for live tax support and advice. Recently Intuit added a service where you perform the low-level labor of entering your data and uploading documents, then a tax expert will review the return and sign as preparer (shifting more accountability and assurance from you onto Intuit). Perhaps this mixture of automation and higher levels of increasingly labor-intensive employee support (for differing price points) might work for your business model.

Designing Your Business Operations

Researchers have proposed a number of theories for helping you think through a logical, efficient, effective design for your business operations. No theory yet developed always provides the optimum solution. Still, they can each assist you when considering each aspect of your operational flow. Listed below in no particular order are the most commonly applied theories for developing operational systems:

Transaction Cost Economics—This theory looks at two major components, (1) search and information costs for each transaction, (2) and policing and enforcement costs. The last one includes legal expenses for stopping vendors or ex-employees from stealing your proprietary products, enforcing pricing and payment terms with vendors and customers, and related issues reflecting uncertainties in conducting business transactions. Sometimes this type of transaction analysis favors in-house production efforts conducted by employees, while at other times the analysis points towards market purchases. This type of analysis is intended to reflect opportunism to maximize profits, whether via minimizing costs or maximizing sale price collections.

Core Competences—Emphasis in this theory is on specialized knowledge, technique, or skill. The combination of specific, collaborative, integrated intellectual assets such as applied knowledge, learned skills, and attitude (some would call emotional intelligence) can create a competitive niche or advantage for a company.

Relational View—According to this theory, operational plans should be based upon strong trusting relationships that promote efficient and cooperative alliances.

Knowledge-based View—Per this theory of operations design, know-how is embedded and carried through multiple entities and channels within and outside a company and its surrounding network. These elements include organizational culture, a company or network's self-identity, policies, routines, documents, systems, employee and leadership attitudes, and similar artifacts that help shape and define both an organization and its operational activities. Developing and refining operational cycles starts from the raw resources available, then proceeds to begin building capabilities utilizing these knowledgeable elements.

Value Matrix—Per this operational theory, the starting point for creating and improving workable activities that accomplish organizational goals begins with mapping features of product or service offerings across business needs. Next, the entrepreneur should define what criteria constitute success.

Resourced-based View—This theory, which may seem similar to the previous Value Matrix approach, begins with considering how the business gathers, combines, and applies resources to achieve a competitive advantage for superior long-term performance. The key to maximizing operational effectiveness and efficiency is through careful management of available resources.

Social Exchange—Based upon a recognition that each person and organization tend to seek self-interest and interdependence, people nonetheless engage in exchanges when such activities yield benefits exceeding related costs. This cost/benefit analysis determines the worth of a relationship. From this viewpoint both the business and society as a whole consist of a series of exchanges.

Evolutionary economics—Predicated upon Darwin's evolution theory as applied to the social sciences, this operational theory claims economic processes evolve over time. It also asserts economic behavior is determined by both individuals and society as a whole (both through peer pressure and police actions). While the macro view of evolution, whether Darwin's original unproven theory or its application to the social sciences has proven false and destructive over long periods of time, this theory includes some truth on a micro or minor change level when applied to individuals. If utilizing this operational theory, a Christian entrepreneur should be careful to keep in mind that truth is unchangeable. Regardless of minor modifications, this approach might provide tweaks to operational performance.

Agency Theory—Perhaps this is the oldest theory explaining operations, both as a business theory and as a legal doctrine. It addresses relationships between business principles[19] and their agents.[20] The firm is thus perceived as a nexus or connection of contractual relationships between hiring authorities and resource holders. Which services should the hiring authority contract for to achieve organizational goals?

Often, entrepreneurs will consider a mix including some or all of these nine theories when designing or developing improvements to business operational cycles.

My goal in writing this book is to provide practical ideas on how to launch and grow a Christian enterprise. In keeping with that objective, I have tried to give you a balance of theories so you can consider the "big picture" while also

---

[19] Entrepreneurs, company owners, investors, etc.

[20] Executives, employees, vendors and others receiving payment for their services.

giving you "street-level" facts and tips. So I will not spend more time expounding on these operational theories beyond the summary overviews I just provided. Hopefully, these summaries along with the practical details in each chapter build the tools you need to succeed in your new enterprise.

Considering the overall topic of automation and outsourcing, you should recognize the kaleidoscope of internal versus outsourced versus automated tasks will change over time as the company grows and market conditions around you evolve.

When should you consider modifications to your operational cycles? Key variables will give you clues. These elements include customer tolerance for changes, differing perceptions of the pricing/quality trade-off, the level of integration with stakeholder staff (vendors, customers, and other non-employees), technology improvements, and changes in international exchange rates, as well Rule of Law stability within and between countries.[21]

Finally, when thinking about outsourcing tasks or contracting with suppliers in other countries, study the level of enforcement (or lack thereof) for private property rights, what Americans refer to as the Rule of Law. Lack of enforcement, almost always accompanied by a culture of governmental and corporate corruption, can seriously hamper outsourcing attempts for fear of theft without any consequences. This is particularly damaging in the area of intellectual property.

---

[21] Particularly if you sell or outsource across national boundaries, as an increasing number of smaller companies are doing today.

The cost of enforcement within Rule of Law nations can also effectively inhibit your outsourcing efforts, particularly regarding sensitive parts manufacturing or services essential to your business survival. Such costs can possibly cause your business to adopt a "trade secret" approach, using multiple suppliers and keeping each unaware of how their portion fits into the entire product, which might be assembled only within your company plant by your own employees. This does not mean you cannot take advantage of outsourcing benefits, but the operational flow might need to be a bit obtuse to minimize the challenges of intellectual property theft.

As with employees, the Biblical approach to vendors should be to seek a healthy relationship, based on mutual trust and respect. When you must sometimes terminate a supplier, especially due to the vendor's violation of contract obligations, be honest as to your reasons. Don't keep them in the dark. That Christ-like approach often leads Christian entrepreneurs to develop stronger supplier relationships. Coordinating your treatment of suppliers and employees for a synergistic benefit to the company allows both stakeholder groups to feel confident about your leadership and your Christian concern for fair dealings with them.

IV

Accounting & Finances

In this section you will explore the accounting area and your financing options.

Chapter 15, 16, 17, and 18 gives entrepreneurs a basic understanding of bookkeeping.

Chapter 19 summarizes non-accounting statistics plus non-traditional accounting and cost-accounting financial data in a summarized management dashboard to give entrepreneurs tools to analyze greater detail when needed.

Chapter 20 goes through the broad categories of taxes and commonly assessed taxes.

Chapter 21 explores the various options you might consider to financing either a for-profit or non-profit corporation and their implications.

15

The 3 Key Financial Statements: The Balance Sheet

Perhaps you have heard the phrase "**debits and credits**." A monk during the Middle Ages, **Luca Bartolomeo de Pacioli** (circa 1447-1517), is credited as the father of accounting. In his book Summa de Arthmetica, Geometria, Proportioni et Propotionalita (1494), he described the double-entry book-keeping system where debits and credits balance each other in every entry made. He also invented the concepts of assets, liabilities, capital accounts, income, and expenses as well as a logical, clear way to present them in the form of a **Balance Sheet** and **Income Statement** (today often referred to as a **Profit or Loss Statement**).

Amazingly, Pacioli also created cost accounting concepts and accounting ethics, plus the **Rule of 72**, a compound interest calculation used to estimate expected investment returns versus potential losses, to determine if a project is worth undertaking. His invention made it easier for business owners to catch theft and waste while providing accurate and timely information on business performance at a level unimaginable in any prior century.

Pacioli's accounting system and financial statements are still the basis of accounting in nearly every nation on earth. So advanced were his ideas that modern accountants have not been able to add much more to Pacioli's ideas, other than including a third financial statement—the **Cash Flow Statement**.

Starting with Pacioli's most simple concept, all entries must balance, with debits (traditionally listed in a left column) equaling credits (listed in a column in the right column). An example would be if you paid $500 to purchase postage stamps. The entry for this transaction would be:

	Debit	Credit
Postage expense	500.00	
Bank checking account		500.00
To record purchase of ten stamp rolls		

You probably noticed the additional note appended after the numerical entries. Months or years later, if you want to know why you spent that money, the note provides a summary explanation. Many low-cost bookkeeping software packages make it easy for you or your company bookkeeper to enter transactions and print out or view reports, plus drill down to see the detail of each and every transaction that composes each number on a financial report.

Introduction to the Balance Sheet

Let's delve deeper into each of the three primary financial statements, beginning with the **Balance Sheet**, which represents the book value of your company's status on one particular day. Think of the Balance Sheet as a snapshot of a moment in time. The top part lists **assets**—what your company owns. The bottom half reflects the liabilities owed and capital—**net worth**. *Assets (debits) should always equal liabilities plus capital balances (both credit balances)*. Amounts listed on the Balance Sheet are historical purchases, not current market value.

Capital balance (also called **equity**) is the net worth (or deficit) based on historical payments. Capital is not the same as the corporate bank balance because some capital might be tied up in "property, plant and equipment"[22] or intangible assets

---

[22] Tangible assets can be referred to as property, plant and equipment (PP&E). Not to be confused with Personal Protective Equipment (PPE) that was recently added to the lexicon. PP&E are frequently tangible, i.e. real world assets, that cannot be easily liquidated. Holding them is usually a good sign of sound financial footing, as the company feels they can hold a significant amount of tangible assets in order to keep the business afloat. A lack of tangible assets, on the other hand, may indicate uncertainty on the part of the company of revenue or the business performance if there is a depressed market outlook.

such as a patent in addition to cash in the bank and accounts receivable due to the company. Still, capital might also be reduced by any bank loans, mortgages, shareholder loans from you, tax payments not yet paid, and any other liabilities.

Balance sheets are further classified by how likely the company will likely convert them to cash within the next 12 months. **Short-term assets** are listed first, followed by **longer-term assets**. Likewise, liabilities due within the next twelve months are listed first as short-term liabilities, with longer-term liabilities stated further down the Balance Sheet.

There are more complicated situations in some balance sheets which we cannot cover in this book without providing several college accounting classes, but hopefully, you understand the basic ideas. To assist you in visualizing how to read a Balance Sheet, below is a sample one that is typical of many smaller businesses:

In double-entry accounting (the concept whereby assets = liabilities + owners' equity) PP&E can be doubly entered as both an asset and a liability as either a debit in one category and a credit in the other, as it represents both categories.

Sample Manufacturers LLC Balance Sheet As of 12/31/20xx		
Assets		
Short Term		
Bank checking	5,023.45	
Accounts Receivable	39,877.50	
Inventory	67,653.99	
Employee Advances	403.00	
Subtotal Short Term Assets		112,957.94
Long Term		
Equipment	109,777.65	
Vehicles	38,001.01	
Accumulated Depreciation	(22,142.33)	
Patents	10,599.00	
Accumulated Amortization	(706.60)	
Subtotal Long Term Assets		135,528.73
Total Assets		248,486.67
Liabilities & Equity		
Short Term Liabilities		
Accounts Payable	12,998.86	
Payroll Taxes Payable	2,247.66	
Bank Line of Credit	90,000.00	
Equipment loan payable – short term portion	12,000.00	
Subtotal Short Term Liabilities		117,246.52
Long Term Liabilities		
Equipment loan payable – long term portion	98,546.42	
Shareholder loan payable	25,000.00	
Subtotal Long Term Liabilities		123,546.42
Total Liabilities		240,792.94
Stockholder Equity		
Capital Stock	200.00	
Retained Earnings	47,493.73	
Dividends	(40,000.00)	
Total Stockholder Equity		7,693.73
Total Liabilities & Equity		248,486.67

Note that the **total assets number** in this example ($248,486.67) equals or balances those debits to the total credits in liabilities and equity. You probably also observed three negative numbers in parenthesis, subtracting from their respective subtotals. Accumulated depreciation and accumulated amortization are book entries. In other words, you do not write a check to get these subtractions. They represent the fact that tangible assets (such as equipment and vehicles) will last and benefit company operations for several years but nonetheless wear out gradually over time. The same concept applies to intangible assets such as patents. These accumulations are "wear and tear" on company assets.

Look again at the **stockholder equity** section. Where is the net profit? Capital stock represents the initial capital infusion you used to start the corporation (i.e., buy stock in your own company). **Retained earnings** is the cumulative amount of net profits, net of prior-year dividend distributions, still retained by the corporation. This year's net profit is included in full with all the other years' net profits not yet disbursed (or net of cumulative deficits in some situations). New entrepreneurs often mistakenly think **dividends** are some sort of expense, which they are not. Dividends are simply a disbursement of some retained earnings during the current year to you as the shareholder, thus reducing the number of earnings retained within the company.

If you started a **nonprofit** charitable organization instead of a for-profit business, the Balance Sheet is compiled in a similar format with a few minor changes, mostly in terminology.

For example, the Balance Sheet is renamed **Statement of Financial Position**. Instead of stockholder equity (since there are no stockholders or owners in a nonprofit organization), the substitute term is **Fund Balance**, some of which might be stated as restricted per donor stipulations. Also, since there are no owners, there can be no dividend payments to nonexistent owners. Also, there will be no loans to or from stockholders, although there might be loans to or from an officer or director in a startup charity.

Insights of the Balance Sheet

Now go back to review the sample Balance Sheet again. What insights does it give you? Understanding all the subtleties in the **United States Generally Accepted Accounting Principles (GAAP)** and **International Financial Accounting Standards (IFAS)** is unnecessary. You do not need to fully understand your bookkeeper's job. However, every entrepreneur should learn how to recognize the insights financial statements give. So let's look at this sample Balance Sheet for our small manufacturing company. There are five issues we should think about from this statement. They are:

1. **Accounts receivable is approximately triple accounts payable.** In other words, we are not financing enough monthly bills with cheap non-interest-charging trade accounts. Any bookkeeping software package you purchase today typically comes with additional reports, two of which are aged receivables and aged payables. These

reports show you the dollar volume of receivables invoiced to customers but still uncollected (or for payables outstanding bills) unresolved for less than 30 days, 31-60 days, 61-90 days, 91-120 days, and over 120 days outstanding. If too many receivables are in the older buckets, you need to improve your collections efforts or risk receivables going stale and uncollectible. You should review the aging reports in this scenario since the triple receivables over payables are costly due to funding your needed operating cash with bank loans rather than the interest-free trade payables.

2. **The bank line of credit (LOC) is approximately $22,000 greater than inventory.** However tempting it may be to fund regular expenses with a LOC draw-down, LOCs are intended solely for financing the cost of goods sold, primarily raw materials purchases until the sale is completed and the receivables collected. Suppose the company cannot keep that discipline. In that case, it is headed for cash flow problems. So as the owner, we should pare down overhead expenses and pay down the LOC (which is a flexible, fluctuating revolving loan tool) until we get it back in line with funding inventory. Keep in mind LOC financing is more expensive than term loans (requiring regular monthly repayments), and is intended for equipment, vehicle, or other long-term asset purchases.

3. **Term loans are 75 percent of equipment and vehicle assets.** On the surface, this looks acceptable. As we review the other two financial statements and the interplay between all three financial statements we will see a need to look at this situation closely. So mark this item as a

caution flag, for now, to explore in more depth later.

4. Why do we have a shareholder loan payable on the Balance Sheet when we paid ourselves enough dividends to pay off this loan? **Most small corporations frequently have shareholder loans sloshing back and forth to either payables or receivables since owner financing is often cheaper than bank financing.** However, there is a potential tax issue related to shareholder loans. A shareholder loan balance will appear on a balance sheet as either an asset or a liability. However, from a tax perspective, if the business or the shareholders treat the shareholder loan as debt, and if the shareholder uses the debt basis to absorb flow-through losses, loan repayment could be subject to capital gains or ordinary income taxes. The IRS tends to more carefully scrutinize this form of loan, as they can be employed as a form of tax avoidance. While banks typically look at cash flow from operations to determine that the amount of cash generated by a company's normal business operations is sufficient to maintain and grow its operations. The opposite (negative cash flow) would require further external financing for capital expansion. When the business is generating enough cash to comfortably cover repayments back to the bank, it is time to do some careful accounting in order to appear fiscally sound to the bank. If the shareholder loans become too high in comparison to stockholder equity the bank might restrict what you can do with your cash flow, reduce your line of credit, increase your interest rate or a combination of these limitations. In this case, a simple book entry will clean up these issues by reducing dividends and reclassifying

$25,000 of dividends to pay off the loan back to ourselves, thus making us look stronger to the banker.

5. **Accumulated amortization is a small amount, implying we recently received a patent for a new product we designed.** That should be a reminder to consider what we are doing to monetize that new patent as swiftly as possible. If that requires greater marketing effort, should we take actions to reshape our next Balance Sheet to encourage the bank towards giving us a working capital loan so we can grow sales faster?

These five points are typical, thought-provoking points a Balance Sheet can focus your attention upon. Probably you will glean fewer ideas from considering your Balance Sheet than from the **Income Statement (Profit & Loss Statement)**. The Cash Flow Statement also tends to yield fewer ideas. But there are brainstorming notions and opportunities to dress up your financial performance to attract financing in all three financial statements, including the Balance Sheet.

16

The 3 Key Financial Statements: Profit & Loss Statement

Income Statements increasingly referred to in many small business bookkeeping software packages as **Profit & Loss Statement**, are like the movie versus the Balance Sheet snapshot. Profit and loss statements show sales and operations performance during some period, typically a month, quarter, or year. Like the Balance Sheet, Profit & Loss Statements can have classifications or grouping of expenses (subtotals) to help you spot issues you should focus on. Consider the following typical sample for a startup manufacturer:

Sample Manufacturers LLC		
Income Statement		
For the 12 months ended 12/31/20xx		
Revenue		
Product line sales	566,980.99	
Replacement parts sales	39,484.00	
Total Revenue		606,464.99
Cost of Goods Sold		
Raw materials		
Machining expenses	249,589.61	
Shop wages	65,000.00	
Freight charges	18,966.12	
Subtotal Long Term Assets		333,555.73
Total Assets		272,909.26
Expenses		
Marketing & Sales		
Advertising	16,257.59	
Manufacturer rep commissions	11,000.00	
Trade show expenses	3,515.00	
Auto expenses	6,509.55	
Travel	8,931.41	
Meals & entertainment	1,786.43	
Bad debts	2,200.00	
Subtotal Marketing & Sales		50,199.98
Office		
Bank charges	1,355.00	
Depreciation & amortization	18,578.00	
Dues & subscriptions	58.00	
Insurance (liability)	6,986.40	
Interest expense	9,143.69	
Legal & accounting	6,150.00	
Office supplies	2,986.55	
Office wages	35,000.00	
Officer salary	50,000.00	
Payroll taxes	9,013.30	
Employee benefits	18,566.00	
Contract labor	6,600.00	
Rent	10,000.00	
Repairs & Maintenance	10,500.99	
Communications	1,899.76	
Utilities	11,856.67	
Subtotal Office		198,694.36
Other		
State & local property & income taxes	1,568.77	
Federal income tax	0.00	
Penalties	35.00	
Subtotal Other		1,603.77
Total Expenses		250,498.11
Net Profit		22,411.15

Again, the **nonprofit** version is similar, using different terminology. Instead of calling this report an Income Statement or Profit & Loss Statement, the nonprofit title is a **Statement of Financial Activities**. Instead of revenue (which some nonprofits have if they sell services or products), income often includes donation income. Instead of Net Profit, that line is called Increase in Net Assets. Or according to the older, more cumbersome term, **Excess of Revenue over Expenses**. Beginning and ending net assets are frequently appended to the bottom of this statement as well. One major difference—which is required on the IRS nonprofit tax return and often reported in financial statements—is a second **Statement of Financial Activities**.

The first version looks similar to the business Profit & Loss Statement with very similar income and expense line items listed. The second version classifies income and expenses by programs the nonprofit undertakes. For example, a charity focused on job training may list income and expenses for inner-city job training and another set for rural poverty area training, as well as separate sets of data for administrative overhead and fundraising efforts.

What messages are this sample Profit & Loss Statement sending to you? There are 11 issues to explore. They are:

1. Accumulated depreciation on the Balance Sheet is $22,142, while this Profit & Loss Statement reflects $18,578 of depreciation and amortization. The

amortization is so low that it most likely represents the first year, so if we subtract, we arrive at $17,871 of depreciation, which is approximately 81% of the accumulated depreciation, clearly representing the first-year write-off. In other words, we purchase new equipment during the year (which we will also see clearly on the Cash Flow Statement). Note our repairs and maintenance cost was $10,501 for the year. The question should immediately pop into your mind to explore why repairs and maintenance should be so high on new equipment, which was probably under warranty during most of this first year. Do we need to conduct shop employees' training, so they know how to handle the equipment properly without causing excessive wear and tear or damage? Do we have attitude problems with one or more employees? If so, this may require a review of our leadership style or a frank discussion with problem employees, using Matthew 18 as a guide to seeking a God-pleasing solution.

2. The Gross Profit of $272,909 is 45 percent of sales. This is a terrific gross profit markup for any American manufacturer! Gross Profit percentage is a very difficult number to improve, unlike Net Profit, which includes many subjective overhead expenses. As good as this looks, how does it compare to our published industry average? If it is significantly higher, competitors will be seeking to knock us off our pedestal; if below the average, why? How does the new patent reflect this? A new patented competitive product advantage should result in a higher Gross Profit percentage than the industry for at least a few years. Is that the case for this first year? If

not, how can we monetize this advantage better over the coming year?

3. Parts sales are approximately 6-1/2 percent of total sales. Are we providing self-service repairs and maintenance to customers? Could we make more if we offered full service, and what costs and reorganization of our operating cycle would be required to efficiently provide such full service? Would such effort generate sufficient profit to be worth the undertaking?

4. Freight is approximately 3 percent of sales. Can bulk contracting with one shipping company cut this cost further?

5. Marketing and sales expenses are around 8.3 percent of sales. Should we boost this expense to promote our new product line more aggressively? Which strategy works best? For example, we paid both direct advertising and independent manufacturers' representatives commissions. Does our direct sales advertising effort undercut the manufacturers' reps' motivation to market our products? How much does the entrepreneur's travel to key customers and trade shows generate in sales? We should explore this area more carefully, especially since marketing and sales costs for many industries often hover near 15 percent of sales—far more than we are currently committing towards building our sales channels. Are we limiting our own growth?

6. Bank fees are low, implying the company requires cash, check, or wire payments from customers, but not credit cards. Merchant fees (the credit card charge banks apply to businesses or merchants for processing customer credit card sales) usually range from 2 percent to 3.1

percent. Would accepting credit cards boost sales sufficiently to be worth the 3 percent reduction in gross profit on such sales? It might be time to conduct a quick customer survey to find out!

7. Legal and accounting expenses are high for this size company, reflecting legal fees related to collections problems. If so, perhaps we should offer a combination of discounts for early payment prior to the due date (often thirty days for most businesses) and a finance charge or late payment charge. Be sure to check your state's regulations and the U.S. Consumer Financial Protection Bureau for any required statements at the bottom of your invoices to be allowed to charge late payment interest charges. If this high expense is due to some other reason, what operational activity should change to keep this cost more reasonable?

8. Interest expense of $9,144 divided by the Balance Sheet total bank debt of $200,546 (line of credit plus short and long term portions of equipment term loan) is approximately 4.6 percent. That is a good interest rate in today's market IF the Balance Sheet debt is an average for the full year. If the loan was taken out late in the year, this interest expense would reflect a much higher interest rate. That is worth investigating. As noted in the Balance Sheet comments, you might want to manage the figures towards producing a more favorable financial picture that would enable you to negotiate a lower interest rate.

9. Office wages and shop wages are only 17.1 percent of all expenses. Service firms typically average around 33 percent of expenses, while manufacturing companies like this often keep labor costs to around 20 percent or

so. It looks like these reflect one office worker and one or two shop guys, all paid modest wages. This might be a good time to review the compensation package versus each employee's productivity to assure we provide an effective combination of motivation and productivity. On the surface, it appears we have good labor efficiency, perhaps from leveraging technology and automation. We also seem to have decent usage of contract or temporary labor to fill in periodic surges in production demand. Yet we should explore how much labor is outsourced in our raw materials purchases from our suppliers. Is it too much, too little, or just right? How we partner with vendors versus bringing in-house or outsourcing more operations affects not only the cost but the speed of delivery to customers and customer satisfaction. In addition, are we risking potential patent violations by outsourcing too much knowledge to our suppliers, or are we protecting our intellectual property sufficiently? Furthermore, is our current compensation plan motivational enough for employees and compassionate enough as Christian entrepreneurs within the constraints of what is affordable for our company performance? Are we supplementing with non-cash compensation, such as time off, company picnic, flex time, etc? Are these supplements building employee motivation and loyalty and presenting a good Christian witness of our values?

10. Utilities are 19.5 percent of sales. This seems high. Assuming the utility meter is working correctly and employee usage is not wasteful, perhaps we need to insulate our plant building—especially if it is a typical small-manufacturer, steel, prefabricated building that tends to

leak large amounts of heat and cooling. The high utility bills are unlikely to be caused by the new equipment. Older equipment often incurs reduced efficiency over time and can raise utility costs somewhat in addition to costing more repairs and maintenance, but that is not our situation in this example.
11. There is no federal tax expense and most likely the state taxes are probably franchise and property taxes rather than state income tax. That indicates the corporation is most likely classified by the IRS and state as an S-corporation (which I will explain more thoroughly in the chapter on taxation). S-corporations are exempt from income taxes on the federal level and by nearly all states with income taxes. Such tax status should raise a couple of questions in our minds. Are the employee benefits mostly contributions to a retirement plan, which in most cases is heavily tilted towards the owner? If not (such as health insurance coverage for employees), we should note to talk with the company insurance agent to review health and other benefits to assure we are purchasing the most cost-effective policies.

Here is a trick question. How much did this manufacturing entrepreneur take home to support his or her family during this sample year? What is the real company profit prior to the entrepreneur's remuneration package? Often entrepreneurs will take advantage of breaks provided in the tax code. In our example, the entrepreneur might have utilized the following tax benefits:

Officer wages	50,000
Employee benefits. Assume all are retirement plan contributions with 80% going to the owner. The remaining amount provides health insurance direct pre-tax cash subsidies to employees only.	14,000
Half of auto expense for fun side trips during business travel	3,255
Hiring a college-aged child to work in the shop for the summer to help subsidize college costs	5,000
Car purchase (annual benefit of depreciating over five years)	7,600
Travel to Board of Directors meetings consisting of family members	4,465
Dividends	40,000
Rent for a building owned by an entrepreneur	10,000
Total remuneration	134,320

It feels great to take home over $134,000 but only pay full tax on the $50,000 wage and partial taxation on the dividends and rent, while the other items are not taxed to the owner. Each year, the challenge is to explain to the banker how much profit the company earned before the company CPA applied the usual tax-reducing strategies that most bankers are aware of, although they are not trained to fully spot them. Therefore it is up to you as the entrepreneurial owner to point out to the banker that the company actually earned more, and you have the discretion to reduce these expenses when necessary, to assure the bank will receive full loan payments during the inevitable periodic lean years.

17

The 3 Key Financial Statements: Cash Flow Statement

Next to explore is our final of the three main financial statements, the **Cash Flow Statement**. There are two acceptable methods for presenting a company's or nonprofit's cash flow. The **Direct Method** (illustrated in this book) shows easily understood summary categories. The **Indirect Method** starts with the Net Profit from the Profit & Loss Statement, then adds adjustments for noncash effects, such as increase or decrease in accounts receivable and payable, depreciation and amortization expenses, change in inventory, and changes in any accrual accounts from the Balance Sheet. Most non-accountant entrepreneurs find the Direct Method easier to understand.

Cash flow statements group changes in cash into three broad categories:

Operating Activities	Reflects the major elements of cash generation and usage during normal (short term) business activities.
Investing Activities	Assets used over multiple years (whether purchased or sold) are included in this group.
Financing Activities	Stock sales, bank loans taken out or repaid, and dividends paid to go into this section.

Nonprofit organizations apply the same three categories, and their cash flow statements look nearly identical to business ones, except for the additional **Reconciliation of Change in Net Assets** to Net Cash Provided by Operating Activities. In effect the nonprofit version displays the Direct Method in the first half, followed by the Indirect Method in the latter half. Any funds restricted by donors or transferred by the Board of Directors to a restricted fund are reflected in the Operating Activities area (if only temporarily restricted) or under Financing Activities (if permanently restricted).

Sample Manufacturers LLC
Cash Flow Statement
For the year ended 12/31/20xx

Cash Flow from Operating Activities		
Cash receipts from customers	622,416.20	
Cash paid to suppliers & employees	(577,554.41)	
Subtotal cash generated from operations		44,861.79
Interest expense paid		(9,143.69)
Tax paid		(1,603.77)
Net cash flow from operating activities		34,114.33
Cash flow from Investing Activities		
Equipment purchases	(120,334.25)	
Proceeds from equipment sales	0.00	
Net cash flow from Investing Activities		(120,334.25)
Cash flow from Financing Activities		
Loan proceeds	102,000.00	
Loan repayments	(18,334.25)	
Bank line of credit net borrowing (repayment)	10,000.00	
Cash dividends paid	(40,000.00)	
Net cash flow from Financing Activities		53,665.75
Net Increase (Decrease) in Cash		(32,554.17)
Beginning Cash		37,577.62
Ending Cash		5,023.45

What messages are this sample Cash Flow Statement sending to you? There are six issues to explore. They are:

1. Operations cash of $34,114 is $11,703 (52 percent) higher than the net profit. In other words, some of the cash is sheltered from taxation by the depreciation and amortization expense, which is a book-entry requiring no cash outlay. This extra cash cushion should be used to save for working capital needs and to eventually replace equipment when it inevitably wears out. But did this entrepreneur rebuild his cash balance?
2. Equipment term loan proceeds represent approximately 85% of the equipment purchased, which is the maximum leverage banks will typically lend. That ratio helps magnify profit, but not necessarily in a positive direction each year. The bank Line of Credit (LOC) exceeds the amount of inventory by over $22,000. Businesses should use LOC proceeds solely for financing inventory purchases until the company receives sales proceeds, not to fund expenses or for asset purchases. This is a problem area we should fix over the coming year to lower the risk of suffering a cash flow crunch.
3. Could leasing equipment instead of buying it has provided more cash flow for use in marketing our new patented products? The faster we can push sales growth rates, the easier it will be to fund investing and financing activities, so this is a topic we should study.
4. Could factoring company receivables have eliminated the cash drawdown? Factoring is a financing technique used by some smaller companies, involving selling receivables

to a factoring company, either with or without recourse. If without recourse, the liability for inability to collect all the receivables is shifted to the factoring company. However, factors do not take on such liability without requiring a significant discount from the face value of the receivables. Yet factoring can be a quick way to generate faster cash collections when the bank, investor, and other financing options are limited, especially in startup firms.

5. The ending cash is only $5,023 versus an average monthly expenditure for suppliers and employees of $48,130 ($577,554/12 months). Thus our ending cash balance represents only three days' worth of funding on hand (5,023/48,130*30 days). This is way too low for safety! As we picked up earlier in this financial statement analysis, the company is overly reliant on the bank line of credit. If the bank realizes this, LOCs can typically be reduced with little to no warning, cutting off available credit, or worse yet, the bank might demand full payment for at least a couple of months each year (called "bring the line to rest") to force the entrepreneur to prove he or she is not overly reliant on borrowed funds to survive a bit longer. What should we do about this potentially dangerous situation? Cut back on owner perks until cash rebuilds to at least the prior year's ending cash balance, representing 23 days worth of average monthly expenses. Better yet, we should build cash gradually up to two months worth of expenses in the bank. There are two reasons why this situation might not be as dire as it appears at first. The first reason is that the demand for our type of products is highly seasonal, and the end of the year happens to be the

lowest demand portion of the year. We can prove this to the bank by providing interim statements (quarterly) and bringing the LOC to rest at the high time of the year. The second reason may be due to the entrepreneur's desire to minimize his personal tax bill. As an S-corporation, the company is exempt from income taxes, but the profit (whether distributed as dividends or not) is tacked onto the shareholder's personal income tax bill. Many small business owners write lots of checks at the very end of the year for expenses while delaying receivables collections until the beginning of the next year. If the company is on a cash basis (which will be explained later in this chapter), the net profit is temporarily reduced to manage a lower tax bill for the year. However, this second reason can be more difficult to convince a banker that it does not reflect cash flow and profitability problems.

6. There are no charitable donations on the Profit & Loss Statement, but the Cash Flow Statement lists $40,000 of dividends paid out. The IRS looks at both the officer salary and the dividends paid in an S-corporation since dividends are free of all payroll taxes. There is no concrete formula for determining the "correct" minimum salary, and entrepreneurs obviously have an incentive to favor dividends to the extent allowed. Many IRS agents question a ratio between salary versus dividends if the salary seems too low and dividends too high. As a Christian, you most likely make significant charitable donations. By making those donations out of the corporation rather than taking dividends first, followed by making personal donations, the benefit of the donations flows through to your personal return

without triggering any audit issues over the high ratio of dividends to salary in this example. Since IRS audits can be costly in time and money, even if you win, it would be more prudent to reconsider using the company to make donations directly.

18

Choosing Your Method

We have now covered the three major financial statements along with examples of the valuable types of insights you should be looking for. Underlying each one of these issues is possible differences in perceptions, attitudes, and maybe employee, vendor, or stockholder conflicts. By analyzing the financial statements carefully you can spot people issues, cash flow challenges, and other concerns when building your company or organization. While accountants usually prepare financial statements to report past history, entrepreneurs review these statements for clues on how to shape the future.

There is another dimension to accounting and financial statements you should understand in order to make sense of your financial statements. How the numbers are entered into your accounting software can make a huge difference. An accrual basis of accounting means you enter transactions when they occur. Cash basis accounting requires entries only when cash is received or disbursed. There are other methods for entering transactions and compiling financial statements, most of which are some hybrid mode of these two foundational theories. The most popular hybrid theory among small American businesses is the income tax method, which is nearly entirely a cash basis except for a limited list of accruals allowed for certain types of expenses.

To illustrate how the three most popular accounting theories for recording transactions can result in different results from the same activities or transactions, consider the following example of a small temporary nursing firm. Suppose the company invoices $ 900,000 in the 12 calendar months of its first year for its consulting services and offers clients up to 30 days to pay. That would mean one month (1/12 of revenues) would be billed this year but not collected until next year. Likewise, assume the entrepreneur contracts with various freelance nurses to help fulfill its contracts, and has received invoices or signed contracts to pay them for work performed with a 30-day delay between receiving their invoices and writing checks to them. Further, let's say the contractors bill the firm $450,000 for the year. Company office rent is a stable $12,000 for the year ($1,000 per month) due and payable the first of each month.

To keep this example simple, suppose the entrepreneur pays himself or herself $100,000 per year, has a payroll tax burden of 10% for the employer portion, and also set up a retirement plan for the sole employee (the entrepreneur) where the company contributes $50,000 annually, sometime after the year-end when all the accounting statements are completed for the year but prior to filing the corporate income tax return. The company also purchases $20,000 worth of computers and office furnishings. To make this illustration a bit more enlightening, perhaps the business owner decides to pre-pay the next two months of office rent before the year-end. The business owner also writes a check to herself or himself for employee business mileage driven during the year of $5,000. She or he dates the check as of December 31 but does not deposit that check from the corporate bank account into the personal bank account until a month or two into the next new year. Finally, the entrepreneur does the same with the contractors, writing checks for the final month of billings early, dated December 31 but mailing them a couple of weeks later (during the next year).

How might these transactions be reflected under each of the three most popular accounting methods (cash, accrual, and income tax basis)? The profit for the firm's first year would be reported as follows:

	Accrual Basis	Cash Basis	Income Tax Basis
Revenue	900,000	825,000	825,000
Expenses			
Contractors	450,000	412,500	450,000
Rent	12,000	12,000	14,000
Officer Salary	100,000	100,000	100,000
Payroll Taxes	10,000	10,000	10,000
Retirement plan contribution	50,000	0	50,000
Depreciation	4,000	4,000	20,000
Auto Mileage Reimbursement	5,000	0	5,000
Total Expenses	631,000	538,500	649,000
Net Profit	269,000	286,500	176,000

Most entrepreneurs want to report on an accrual basis to their banker (which unlike this example normally results in the highest profit reported) but use the income tax basis for their tax returns, and run the business day-to-day on a cash basis. Each approach has its strengths and weaknesses. Under **US Generally Accepted Accounting Principles (GAAP)** you are free to choose which method you feel works best for you, but then you are expected to continue reporting on the same basis for many years. If you switch, you must let the bank know. The Internal Revenue Service requires you to obtain their prior permission before changing accounting basis methods unless you meet certain automatic change approval situations, which generally cause (or force) your taxable income to be higher.

Suppose your banker or investors require you to pay a **Certified Public Accountant (CPA)** to prepare formal financial statements so the bank or investors can feel more confident about the company's financial performance. A CPA will typically prepare footnotes! Always read the footnotes. They contain valuable information about the known and unknown factors affecting company performance. It is typically where an auditor will immediately look for any red flags.

These footnotes explain several items including:

1. The basis of accounting you are using
2. Reflection of significant disclosures, such as the basis for calculating any estimates
3. Depreciation methods
4. Any known events that might affect the material presented in the statement that would occur between the period covered in the statement and date the CPA issues the statement
5. Obligations not reflected in the financial statements (such as future lease obligations or unused lines of credit)

If you have accepted investor funds you are most likely subject to mandatory government regulatory reporting to the **Securities and Exchange Commission (SEC)** and state securities commissioners. These reports require more extensive reporting than the GAAP footnotes in the CPA-prepared financial statements. Such additional requirements can include revenue segments or major market niches, risk factors, and management expectations about the company's future.

When the CPA prepares a set of financial statements, the CPA firm will issue a formal opinion on the statements as one of the following:

- **Qualified**—in other words, some of the numbers are uncertain or doubtful as to accuracy.
- **Unqualified**—in other words, what you are aiming for every time.
- A "**going concern**"—in other words, the CPA is unsure if your company will survive another year or not.

There are three levels of assurance a CPA firm can express to your financial backers. They are:

Compilation	The CPA took your numbers but did not verify their accuracy.
Review	Some limited procedures were performed to provide a modest level of assurance that the financial figures are probably correct or close.
Audit	Your CPA performed extensive (though not exhaustive, prohibitively expensive) tests to verify the numbers present a fair and likely accurate portrayal of the company's performance and situation. Note the audit opinion states the numbers are "fairly stated," not precise, and there is no opinion stated about whether your company suffered any fraud, waste or has sufficient internal controls to prevent such problems.

You have several important accounting decisions to make. What would be the most helpful basis of accounting to manage your company? What level of assurance do your banker or investors require to feel comfortable with the financial performance you give them, yet keep the CPA fees affordable for the stage your company has grown to thus far? Should you pay for the full footnote disclosures, or will your financiers permit you to save some money by skipping some or all of the footnotes? In other words, what are your goals (minimizing taxes, tracking cash flow, etc.) versus the uses your financial statement users seek (bankers, investors, perhaps mid-level managers, etc.)?

Also, keep in mind that your accounting software reports will probably work just fine for supervisors or managers working for you and for your own usage throughout the year. Formal statements from a CPA are usually prepared once a year (if at all) for closely held companies or quarterly if you have SEC filing requirements. Differing accounting reports should be designed for various users to meet each type of user's diverse needs.

19

Dashboards & Ratios

The modern concept of operational cycles within a company grew in popularity. Sophisticated reporting software spread from large companies down to very small and startup firms. Now, even low-cost accounting software packages build in the ability to report non-accounting information and other financial data besides traditional financial statements.

These packages also often allow integration with other software, such as payroll, production, or customer management, and give you the ability to export data into spreadsheets and other software for further data analysis. They even allow you to merge financial figures with non-financial statistics. Accounting software that builds in such capabilities provides a summary or overview of your company in a format or screen referred to as a **dashboard**.

All data listed on the dashboard are summaries. Entrepreneurs can click on a statistic or report to drill down into several layers of detail. For example, two common summaries are aged accounts receivable and aged accounts payable. They display total dollar figures that are compiled into groups of every 30 days, such as less than 30 days, 31 to 60 days old, 61 to 90 days old, 91 to 120 days old, and more than 120 days old.

Dashboards can often be set to include various accounting ratios. Formats can include figures for the current month and year-to-date or a graph of ratio trends over the current year and sometimes compared to the prior year. There are many accounting ratios. The following is a list of the most popular ratios utilized by startup entrepreneurs:

Current Ratio

Calculated as current (or short-term) assets divided by current liabilities.[23] This ratio reflects the company's ability to generate sufficient cash flow to cover obligations within the coming twelve months. A ratio of 2.0:1 or greater is considered a healthy situation.

Quick Ratio

It is calculated as liquid assets[24] divided by current liabilities. This ratio gauges the company's ability to quickly liquidate cash-like assets into cash and use the money to pay off bills

---

[23] See the Balance Sheet in chapter 13 for the types of assets that are included under current or short-term.

[24] Cash, marketable securities, and accounts receivable.

in a hurry. The big difference between the current and quick ratios is inventory. It is assumed to take a while to sell, so it is excluded in the quick ratio calculation. A healthy quick ratio would be 1.0:1, indicating you could pay for emergencies, such as equipment repairs, storm damage, or other surprises.

Inventory Turnover Ratio

The **inventory turnover ratio** is calculated as the cost of goods sold divided by average inventory. Average inventory is calculated by adding the beginning and ending inventory for the period then dividing it in half. This ratio discloses how frequently you are able to convert inventory into sales, so the company does not tie up money invested in inventory. It is one measure of efficiency. The higher the ratio, the more frequently you can convert or turn inventory into sales. A "good" ratio depends on the product you sell. For example, a home builder might achieve a turnover of 1.5:1 during a year while a retail Internet seller of household products might reach a 5:1 ratio (all the inventory sold or turned over five times throughout the year).

ROI

This term refers to **Return On Investment (ROI)**, which is calculated as Net Profit minus your investment in assets (in other words your Net Worth or Stockholder Equity). This calculation is referred to as **Net Return on Investment**. The

Net Return on Investment is then divided by the cost[25] to arrive at a percent return. A healthy ROI depends greatly upon the type of asset you are considering and how much leverage (loan financing) you obtain.

Debt to Equity Ratio

Banks and other lending sources often allow small business owners to achieve high amounts of debt relative to their book basis net worth in the company after the entrepreneur proves they can pay the debt. The **debt to equity ratio** is calculated simply as debt divided by equity. Most startup businesses that are earning positive cash flow have high ratios in the early years, which decline to more normal leverage ratios of 2:1 to 4:1 after a few years.

Times Interest Earned Ratio

Perhaps a more helpful ratio that your lender will monitor closely is **Times Interest Earned Ratio**, calculated as net profit before interest expense and income taxes divided by the interest expense. This displays how much of a cushion the bank or lender has for collecting its interest, or how much coverage your company can produce. A variation on this ratio is the **Times Debt Earned Ratio**, in which the divisor includes both the interest expense plus the principal debt payments. This ratio shows how easily your company can cover loan

---

[25] What you paid for the asset, not any portion financed with loans.

payments. Healthy ratios for interest and for debt are typically 2.5:1 or greater and 1.5:1 or greater, respectively.

Accounts Receivable Turnover Ratio

Accounts Receivable Turnover Ratio is calculated as credit (non-cash) sales divided by average accounts receivable. Average means adding the beginning and ending receivables balances then dividing them in half, similar to the inventory turnover ratio calculation. While inventory turnover exhibits your skill at selling your entire inventory quickly multiple times throughout the year, the accounts receivable turnover ratio demonstrates your ability to collect those sales and convert them to cash expeditiously.

You can find many other accounting ratios in accounting textbooks or on the Internet, but these are most of the primary financial health indicators for a small business.

You may also want to track an additional critical ratio on your dashboard. The **Gross Profit Margin** is calculated as Gross Profit (sales minus cost of goods sold) divided by sales. Each industry has a gross profit margin against which you may measure your own performance.

The **Net Profit** margin is not very helpful to most entrepreneurs because the numbers are easily manipulated to minimize taxes or when the timing of expenses varies significantly, especially when recorded on a cash or income tax basis. But Gross Profit is very difficult to change much, so this is a critical figure to track. If it begins to slip you know you are in trouble.

If you operate a service business, do not be fooled into thinking you lack a Gross Profit. Your "cost of goods sold" consists of wages, contract labor, payroll taxes on that labor, and fringe benefit plans provided to those workers for whom you bill clients, such as consulting.

The old **Rule of Thirds** still holds true for most smaller service businesses. This rule sets a goal of one-third of revenue should cover direct costs (your cost of goods sold, leaving a 67 percent Gross Profit Margin). Another third should cover all your overhead. The final third should be profit.

Dashboards

Dashboard indicators might also include **cost accounting statistics** if you are a leading manufacturing business. Cost accounting involves tracking against "standard" or expected costs for each step in your manufacturing process. Variances (either positive or negative) could be shown on your dashboard for each step in your operational process so you can swiftly and precisely spot inefficiencies developing and where.

In addition to all these dollar figures and perhaps some time figures, such as how long production or inventory is sitting in your shop, **dashboards** can include statistics from other areas of your operations:

- From a human resources viewpoint, you might want a warning indicator on the amount of overtime worked and worker time missed.
- Marketing indicators might pull in summaries from customer servicing software to reflect the number of prospect calls made per week, prospect inquiries, discounts offered to sell products or services, and other marketing statistics.
- Operational statistics might better be graphed rather than list figures so you can easily see time delays or changes in production speeds for each step in your operational process.
- **Benchmarking** is a concept where you compare each key indicator for your own company against the industry averages. There are multiple sources of industry benchmark statistics. Some small business-oriented websites offer industry data, such as www.bisworld.com or www.bizstats.com, and you can probably find more statistics plus help to locate that information at the reference desk of your local library. In addition, some business brokers are willing to share industry averages for your area, and CPAs are always a great source of such knowledge as well as how to set up your dashboard to provide the most critical measurements for your company.

The overall purpose of the dashboard is to provide you, the top-level entrepreneurial leader, a summary of the key pulse items in your business. The design should then let you drill down to explore any statistics which vary significantly (either good or bad) so you can fix problems and boost improvements. With the mix of historical accounting and other data plus projections, you have the tools to focus on improving future company performance.

Whether you launch a nonprofit organization or a for-profit business as a Christian, you probably want to include some measurements on your dashboard tracking progress towards **non-financial objectives** in the areas of social welfare, environment, and spiritual goals. Progress in these areas can be very difficult to determine. We will cover these areas later in this book. For now, keep in mind the idea of including some measurements for these other goal areas of your business on your dashboard.

20

Choosing Your Business Entity

Taxes and legal structure issues overlap. Over the next two chapters, we will provide overviews for both areas. Keep in mind there are many nuances so it is essential you seek professional advice before structuring your legal and tax organization. Information in this chapter gives you an overview but is not intended to be legal and tax advice for your specific situation.

There are five main categories of legal structure, and most have variations of each type. To complicate issues more, each nation has different filing requirements, and some countries' registration requirements can be very lengthy and expensive. In this chapter, we will review the major components from a United States law viewpoint. All of these formations are state issues. There is no federal or national business formation, with the extremely rare vote of Congress to form a special nonprofit or other corporation. Nearly all businesses in the United States are formed by filing formation documents with a state Secretary of State office, and nearly all of these state agencies now provide easy "fill-in-the-blanks" legal forms.

Sole Proprietorship

This form of business organization is the easiest one to set up. Simply announce to potential customers that you are now in business! Sole proprietorships require no registration with any government entity for formation and no paperwork you must keep to maintain this status. In addition the sole proprietorship is included as part of your personal income tax return. However, some towns and counties require an annual business license for all types of businesses, including a sole proprietorship.

Advantages are obvious. This form of business is effortless to create and maintain from a government filing perspective. The huge disadvantage is this form of business organization provides no liability protection.

Partnership

Partnerships have multiple owners. **General partnerships** require no government filing to form or maintain, although some towns and counties require a business license for every type of business. The general partnership has no legal paperwork requirements at all, but it is wise to prepare a written partnership agreement that all partners sign to avoid future disputes. The big disadvantage to a general partnership is each partner is fully liable for all partnership debts incurred by every partner with no limitation.

Limited partnerships are similar to general partnerships with a few very important differences. Many states require registration with the Secretary of State, which typically provides online forms to create a limited partnership. There is also an annual report required by the Secretary of State to preserve the limited partnership. Each limited partner has limited liability up to the value of their capital account in the partnership. However, there must be at least one general partner who has unlimited liability exposure.

A special category of partnership is the **professional limited liability partnership (PLLP)**. This entity is limited to licensed professionals in the same profession, such as all partners must be lawyers or all must be medical doctors. For this organizational form there still must be at least one general partner with unlimited liability. In addition, in a professional partnership, even the limited partners can be held to unlimited liability for professional service errors or malpractice committed by either themselves or their partners.

You can create different classes of limited partners—but not general partners. Each class can be entitled to participate at differing levels of profits and losses as well as varying voting rights in partnership decisions. Professional firms tend to create income partners, similar to a fixed salary but not classified as employees, rather than equity partners, who must contribute additional capital to buy into the equity class and have full voting rights, leadership possibilities, and participation in profits as a percentage rather than a fixed dollar amount.

Unincorporated associations, sometimes used for organizing a nonprofit, can be classified as tax-free, but that does not limit the liability for members. Unincorporated associations are often viewed as general partnerships for liability purposes, but state law treatment varies.

Corporations

A corporation is the first type of entity to provide complete liability protection for owners. Forming a corporation requires completing **Articles of Incorporation** and filing them with your chosen state's Secretary of State. It also requires a designated **Registered Agent**. If you form the company in the state where you live, you can be the Registered Agent. If you choose to charter the corporation in a state other than the one you live in—which you are welcome to do—you will need to have a Registered Agent in that state. There are a number of registered agent companies that provide such a service at a modest cost. The Secretary of State will also require filing an annual report to maintain the charter in almost all situations.

Over the years, states have created several types of corporations. The **general corporation** is an all purpose model. Many states offer a **nonprofit model** that may or may not have members, and in some cases, stockholders like the general for-profit version. A third type of corporation is the **privately**

held company.[26]   Nearly all corporations are required to produce bylaws, which are detailed laws or rules for that particular corporation detailing how the company handles issues such as issuing stock, holding board meetings, officer duties and how they are appointed, when notices of meetings must be sent and similar issues. Corporations must also keep stockholder ledgers and issue stock certificates (unless the corporation is a nonprofit with no stockholders or members), and the corporation secretary must keep minutes of both stockholder meetings and board of directors meetings which must be held each year. Those states offering the closely held corporation charter allow the incorporator (the entrepreneur or person forming the company) to eliminate these paperwork requirements if there are only one or a few stockholders.

Corporations can have multiple classes of both common stock and preferred stock. The word "**preferred**" refers to a preference to receive dividends before any common stockholders can. On the other hand, preferred stockholders almost never are allowed to vote for board members, while common stockholders generally do vote.

A very recent phenomenon is the **B corporation**, offered by only a few states thus far. This corporation is chartered as a socially conscious corporation. The intent is for the corporation to pursue profit like a regular corporation but also spend resources on socially helpful causes. Stockholders in a B corporation are prohibited from suing the board or officers for failure to maximize return on investment for the shareholders,

---

[26] Some people may also call it a closely held corporation.

as would be the case for a regular corporation.

The B corporation is intended to be a hybrid between a profit-making business and a charity. Practically speaking, any business can elect to pursue triple bottom line goals and B Corporation certification. The **B Rating System** is a certification program conducted by B Lab, derived from a survey of 60 to 170 questions on community, environment, and consumer interactions. A third-party firm audits the applicant to determine whether the company portrayed its social conscience efforts accurately. For the majority of triple bottom line (social and environmental) goal measurements an independent audit or certification firm verification process is required. You can explore a free B-corporation assessment tool at BimpactAssessment.net.

This confused type of entity can make bankers nervous to lend. Note: there is no prohibition on an entrepreneur pursuing social causes alongside profit-making in a regular corporation.

Limited Liability Company

The limited liability company, commonly referred to as LLC, is a European invention intended to be a mix between a limited partnership and a corporation. It has the limited liability advantages for every "**member**" (the term is the equivalent of a partner or shareholder) but none of the paperwork requirements to keep minutes or a membership ledger or any other paperwork. To form an LLC you would use the form provided by the Secretary of State in the state you wish to create it. This form is called Articles of Organization—similar to the corporation's Articles of Incorporation but with far more flexibility. The Secretary of State will require filing an annual report to maintain the LLC.

You have the option to issue member certificates (the equivalent of stock certificates in a corporation) and keep minutes, but there is no minimum number of meetings required each year. The LLC is not required to have any "**bylaws**" (called **Operating Agreement**) but if you intend to have multiple owners it is a good idea to draft the rules under which disputes between members can be quickly resolved. LLCs can have officers with any title you wish, unlike the somewhat limited list of officer titles for a corporation. Typically the LLC equivalent of a corporate president is called a manager in the LLC. The LLC may have one manager or a board of managers (roughly equivalent to the corporation's board of directors) but neither a manager nor a board of managers is required. It can be run directly by the members if you wish, similar to a general partnership. You can also create endless classes of members, each with different legal rights and participation in profits.

Business Trust

Business trusts have been around for a long time but are not very popular. These entities are created by a legal document called a **trust indenture** or **declaration of trust**. A business trust can be created by anyone as a private document governing how the trust will operate, somewhat similar to the LLC Operating Agreement. Some states permit registration of the trust. Instead of a stockholder or member the person contributing capital and other assets is called a **grantor**. Replacing the officers and board of directors from a corporation the business trust has one or more trustees. The final entity is the **beneficiary**, who is entitled to enjoy any profits or assets distributed. Note the Grantor and beneficiary split the equivalent role of stockholder in a corporation.

The Liechtenstein Trust

This section on types of business formation has focused only on American entities. Nearly all nations have equivalent entities which American tax authorities will recognize and treat similar to domestic status – with one exception. Two nations in the world—Liechtenstein and Panama—offer creation of a **Liechtenstein Trust.**

Under the law of these two nations, this type of trust is considered a charitable trust with owners, grantor, trustees, and beneficiaries of two classes. Those owning or entitled to assets can be different from those receiving cash (**beneficiaries**). Control of the trust can be very complicated. The two classes of beneficiaries can be what most people would think of as traditional charity-type entities or causes, but the other class can be family members.

The Liechtenstein Trust is too complicated and too different in organization for the IRS to classify it according to United

States tax classifications. It has no domestic equivalent in American law. So the IRS considers all of it a business trust, and calls owners beneficiaries. States have either not taken a position on this type of entity or have conflicting treatment of it. None recognize the charitable or partial charitable status accorded in some of the other nations. As an American citizen operating an American business, if you expand internationally, this type of entity should be avoided in most situations.

Because each of these entities is formed under a single state's law, when you expand your business into another state you are required to register as a **foreign company** in that new additional state. **Domestic companies** are those formed within the current state. Foreign companies are those formed in another state and now registering in a state other than their state of formation. **Alien companies** are those formed in other nations and now registering in a particular state. Obviously, each filing for formation or registration requires paying the Secretary of State a modest fee each year.

Specific Problem Areas for Your Business Entity

Each type of entity has certain problem areas to watch for. **S corporations** are scrutinized by tax agents to assure the amount of wages taken by shareholders is reasonable versus the more tax-advantaged dividend distributions of profits. For **C corporations** IRS agents look at the opposite, whether officer salaries are too high and tax advantaged fringe benefits too rich. If you form a **nonprofit organization**, state and federal tax agents will want to know what related-party transactions you engage in between yourself, family members, and for-profit companies you own with your tax-exempt organization.

What Kind of Business Entity Should You Choose?

For perspective, it's good to know under what circumstances most entrepreneurs utilize these different types of entities. Very small companies that intend to stay small may find the **sole proprietorship** and **partnership** forms easiest to use. In addition, if you hire your own children as minors in a sole proprietorship you can shift their income to children's college savings accounts through paying them wages for work they help you with, while avoiding payroll taxes until the children turn age 18. Hiring a spouse in a sole proprietorship can also save tax money on fringe benefit plans that can cover you as the entrepreneur, though you will still need to pay payroll taxes on spousal wages.

Most small businesses are taxed as **S corporations**. Though any tax benefits of fringe benefit plans for officers are unfortunately neutralized for shareholders/officers, there is one big benefit: the ability to distribute some profits as dividend distributions. This eliminates any payroll and self-employment taxes on those distributions.

Larger businesses and those where the entrepreneur wants to take advantage of many fringe benefit plans (group life insurance, health insurance, child care, etc.) on a pre-tax basis will be filing as a **C corporation,** or **C-corp** for short. The big drawback to C-corp status is any dividends are double taxed. However, if the company has always been classified as a C-corp (not switched status throughout the years) then when you sell it a substantial portion of the sale price can be tax free, subject to several restrictions and conditions in the tax code.

LLCs are deemed the ultimate tax tool for many entrepreneurs because of their immense flexibility. For example, it is common for nearly all startup businesses to lose money in the first year or two. If the LLC is classified as either a sole proprietorship or partnership, tax losses can be deducted without limit in most situations. Then when the LLC begins making money you can switch the tax status to S-corp status to save taxes on profit distributions. The LLC is the only type of entity that allows these changes in income tax status without changing federal and state tax identification numbers and re-registering for all the other types of taxes.

For charitable and **nonprofit organizations**, most of which are now organized as **corporations**, there is more disclosure required, but also more flexibility. You can offer tax deductions to donors and operate a business without paying taxes as long as the business is directly related to the charitable purposes of the organization. You, as the founder, can take a salary and fringe benefits.

An Example

Here is an example to consider: One of my clients set up a charitable foundation to promote self-employment among poorer rural and urban residents while preserving the environment. The foundation teaches these low-income people how to start and operate agribusinesses that either harvest, transport, or sell certain crops. The foundation qualifies to receive grant money and donations from agribusinesses looking for suppliers or customers the foundation is training.

In addition, the foundation has affiliated for-profit partners from whom the foundation earns business income directly related to creating job opportunities for disadvantaged people in the agribusiness sector while preserving land. Landowners of extensive property can periodically donate land or conservation easements for tax deductions, which the foundation can then rent to the harvesting companies it is helping to create. Entire impoverished communities are uplifted with new job creation, more economic activity, and connections with companies they can do business with. At the same time, the foundation generates several income streams, all tax-free, to support its mission. And can even pay the nonprofit entrepreneur well!

21

Taxes and Regulations

At the end of the previous chapter, we saw a good example of how fuzzy the line is between for-profit businesses and a non-profit charity which applies creative income ideas. Consider a for-profit corporation, sole proprietorship, or partnership that makes charitable contributions and hires some unneeded labor to give those people training and help, or which gives away some product to poor members of the community as part of its Biblical witness in the community. What is the difference between such for-profit businesses and nonprofit charitable corporations? Nonprofit charities must generate income to stay in operation. The point is that choice of entity and tax election is not as sharp a line as many people think. In addition, some entrepreneurs start several corporations, one of which might be registered as tax-exempt, to achieve all their goals.

Now that you have formed your business entity you will:

1. Register to pay taxes.

2. Receive various tax identification numbers from the Internal Revenue Service (IRS for federal taxes).
3. Receive state taxes from each state's Department of Revenue.
4. Receive each state's Employment Security Commission or equivalent agency to pay state unemployment taxes.
5. Some municipalities and counties also have licensing requirements.

What kind of taxes should you expect?

At a minimum, you will need to file **separate income tax** returns for all types of businesses—except the sole proprietorship. This is included in your personal income tax return.

Partnerships file a **form 1065** partnership return, which passes the income through to each partner on a **K-1 form**[27] so partners can report and pay tax on their share of the partnership profits, both for income tax and self-employment (Social Security tax for the self-employed) purposes.

Business trusts can file as either a partnership (form 1065) or a trust (form 1041). Depending upon how the business trust indenture was designed, the trust will either pass profits through to beneficiaries on a different type of K-1 form, or

---

[27] Schedule K-1 is an Internal Revenue Service (IRS) tax form issued annually for an investment in a partnership. The purpose of the Schedule K-1 is to report each partner's share of the partnership's earnings, losses, deductions, and credits.

the trust will pay taxes like a corporation, but at higher rates.

Corporations would usually file a form 1120 corporate tax return. This is called a **C corporation**, or **C-corp** for short, named for the code section of federal tax law governing corporate taxation. However, if there are a limited number of shareholders (100 or less) the shareholders can elect to exempt the corporation from federal (and often state) income taxes. This election, called a **S corporation election**, or **S-Corp** for short, lets the corporation file a different type of return on **form 1120S** which passes the profits through to the shareholders on a different type of **K-1 form**, to be included on their personal tax returns.

LLCs are different. As noted before, the LLC was invented in Europe. As American states began to adopt this type of formation law, the IRS could not find a corresponding entity classification in American tax law. Thus, LLC owners can select any of the standard tax classifications:

- Sole proprietorship — only a single member or husband and wife owners.
- Partnership.
- C-corp or S-corp status.
- Trust status — in very limited circumstances.

The LLC can also change tax status without forming a new entity. This gives LLCs huge flexibility.

To make an election rather than letting the IRS choose a default classification for you, the company must file form

8832 Entity Classification Election. It must also form **2553 Election by a Small Business Corporation** if you also want to claim **S-corp** status).

Finally, **nonprofit** entities, regardless of the type of state law formation, all file one of the **form 990 series** of forms. As tax-exempt entities most would not owe any income tax. However, if a nonprofit earns profits from a business that is unrelated to its primary purpose the charity or other type of nonprofit will owe income taxes—called **Unrelated Business Taxable Income or UBTI tax**—at the corporate income tax rate. Obtaining **tax-exempt status** is not an easy task. You must apply to the IRS on **form 1023**, include your organizational charter with two specific articles included, and usually respond to one or more rounds of additional IRS sets of questions. Just because your state issues you a "nonprofit corporation" charter does NOT mean the IRS—or even your own state tax department—will honor that status until the IRS issues approval via a form letter called a **determination letter**.

Here are some points to consider:

- Federal law calculates income tax as a net profit basis.
- Several states have no income tax.
- Check with your state tax department.
- Some states known widely to have no personal income tax still have a business tax, such as Florida and Tennessee.
- Others that have no income tax may assess a franchise tax (which is a tax on the right for an entity to continue

existing another year).
- States with income taxes also include franchise taxes on their income tax returns.
- Some states use a gross rather than a net method of taxation on income or revenue, and all that have income taxes offer widely differing plethora of incentive credits.

If you operate in multiple states you may find the conflicting state income tax laws can sometimes create duplicate taxation of some profits. To add to the confusion, some states will not recognize the S-election pass-through status for state income tax purposes. Even when an entity such as an LLC is ignored for federal and state tax purposes, a state may choose to require a special LLC tax return and tax, such as California imposes.

Payroll Taxes

Income taxes tend not to be the major nemesis of most small business owners. **Payroll taxes** require frequent tax payments—several times per month for many smaller companies—and quarterly federal tax return filings to the IRS. In addition, states require either monthly or quarterly **income tax withholding** tax returns and quarterly **unemployment tax returns**, plus a year-end reconciliation of the monthly income tax **withholding returns**.

Year-end reports include **W2** wage statements to each employee, a **W3** summary form for all the W2s, all submitted to the Social Security Administration, plus a **federal unemployment tax return** submitted to the IRS. With so many payroll tax filings and frequent multiple filing and payment deadlines every month, most smaller businesses turn to a payroll tax company to administer all the payroll-related tax payments and filings for a modest fee.

Some payroll-related taxes are not handled by payroll services. These would include city privilege licenses and occupational licenses where the rate is based upon the number of employees. A few states also impose a tax for short-term disability benefits, family leave taxes, and other miscellaneous labor-related local taxes.

VAT and Sales Taxes

Sales taxes and value-added taxes (VAT) are often confused but are distinctly different. We will define and explain them below.

VAT taxes—which stands for **Value Added Tax**—have not yet appeared in the United States (except for a brief few years in Michigan), although the VAT is far more popular than the sales tax among foreign governments. The idea behind the VAT is to tax each and every level of transaction on both products and services. In this case, the end-user, however, is infrequently taxed. Input and output credits must be tracked by businesses to claim any credit for VAT taxes paid at a prior level. While the VAT tax is passed on to the price paid ultimately by the end-user, there are additional bookkeeping costs incurred to track input and output credits at each stage, and the net effect is a price increase at every level—much higher in total than sales tax.

Sales taxes are imposed only on the final user of the product. Few states tax services, and none currently tax sales by manufacturers and wholesalers to retail stores. Only the final customer at the retail store or any retail sales made by wholesalers and manufacturers are subject to sales tax.

Use Tax

A related type of tax is called the **use tax**. It is imposed on the user rather than the retail seller and is designed to pick up tax on all retail product transactions by filling in any gap between seller and user if they are in different states. A recent Supreme Court ruling has also allowed any state to collect sales tax from most smaller companies, even if they have no presence (called **nexus**) in another state. If you sell tangible products to end-users or buy products under a sales tax exemption, you will be required to file monthly or quarterly sales tax returns in each state you sell to if you meet each state's minimum threshold under the Supreme Court's Wayfair vs. State of South Dakota ruling.

Personal Property Tax

Another type of tax is the **personal property tax**. Personal property taxes are **Tangible Non-Real Estate Assets** in respect to any person. For example, business equipment such as computers, printers, desks, chairs, and other office assets are all personal business property, since they are not attached to a building or land. Business personal property taxes are usually imposed by counties, although some states such as Ohio impose state-level as well as county personal property taxes on business assets.

Customs Reports and Duties

If you are importing parts or products from other nations your business will also need to file and pay **customs reports** and **duties**. Customs duties are taxes on anything imported into the United States. If you sell to customers in other nations you will need to become familiar with the other countries' customs duties, taxes, and fees, as well as requirements for clearing both United States customs offices and foreign customs ports. For many smaller businesses, this is a good area to outsource for a **customs broker** to complete for you.

Transfer Pricing

Should your business continue to grow internationally, another area of tax law to understand is **transfer pricing.** The concept behind transfer pricing is that tax authorities around the world are concerned that you might set up a subsidiary in a low tax jurisdiction and allocate a disproportionate amount of the profit between your USA company and the low tax company to minimize American taxes, foreign taxes, or taxes overall among all nations where you conduct business.

A **transfer pricing agreement** with the IRS and other nations' taxing authorities attempts to make advanced justifiable allocations rules of price markups when you sell between two companies, and you own both sides of the transaction. There is a lack of coordination between nations on the transfer pricing issue, so it is possible to be taxed on more than 100% of profits.

Tax Audits and Tax Collection

In addition to filing and paying these categories of taxes throughout the year, you will find it necessary to address **tax audits** and **tax collection** issues. Every small business at some point runs into one or more of these challenges. Tax audits can come from a variety of local, county, state, and federal tax agencies and can consume a substantial amount of time. To brace for such times you should keep your accounting records for seven years as well as your bookkeeping general ledgers and financial statements. Also, find a good CPA to protect you. It almost never pays for an entrepreneur to attend a tax audit or collections hearing themselves or to accompany their CPA. You will obtain better results from hiring a CPA with audit and collections experience.

Information Returns

You will also have to pay all the types of taxes businesses are required to file various **information returns**. The most common is the **1099-MISC** form due to both the IRS and each contract laborer or vendor you pay $600 or more to throughout the year, unless the vendor is a nonprofessional or general corporation. Not only are there penalties, but you might also owe up to 30% of the amounts you paid the supplier during the year if you fail to file this form and the accompanying **1096** "cover sheet" type form. Penalties can still be assessed if you do not have proof the supplier is not subject to backup withholding.

You can get protection against this assessment by asking upfront for the vendor or contractor to sign a **W9 form**, which gives you all the data you will need to complete a **1099-MISC** for the supplier at the end of the year plus gives you their signature certifying they are not subject to the backup withholding rules. If they were not truthful about that, the signed W-9 form makes you bulletproof against paying your supplier's taxes for him or her.

An increasing number of states are requiring businesses to file the equivalent of the federal 1099-MISC if you pay a vendor located outside the state and withhold a percentage of what you pay that vendor. Check your state department of revenue to determine if your company must comply with such a rule.

Missed tax payments

Missed tax payments will result in tax notices as well as assessments for penalties and interest. It is best to request waivers of penalties every few years and pay the other notices you receive in between those times.

Do not ignore collections notices. Not only can penalties and interest pile up rapidly, but the IRS and state also have the ability to drain your bank account, seize assets, shut down your business, and in egregious circumstances put you in debtor prison without the benefit of a trial, in some states. Liens filed against you can hurt your credit rating and cause your bank to demand full repayment immediately on your business lines of credit.

Trust Fund Taxes

One particularly dangerous area for small business owners is what the IRS and states call **trust fund taxes**. These are payroll taxes withheld from employees but not yet paid to the government.

If you formed a corporation or LLC the tax authorities have great difficulty piercing your corporate limited liability shield for company taxes. But payroll taxes withheld from your employees are assumed to be a de facto trust with you as trustee personally liable and the government as the beneficiary. This fictitious or assumed trust can be financially deadly for you personally as well as your business.

Therefore if you are short on funds, which happens periodically to all business owners, and you are unable to borrow to cover the shortfall, the best solution is to prioritize. *Pay the trust fund taxes first.* Government agents will be more willing to work out payment plans on any other taxes except trust fund taxes from payroll withholdings.

Labor Law and Safety Law Requirements

In addition to taxes, there are a number of non-financial impositions to watch. For example, the **Occupational Health & Safety Administration (OSHA)** can fine a business $7,000 per violation for any unsafe working environment infractions. This might include not having all the required federal and state labor law posters displayed where employees can read them. Federal agencies do not coordinate the posters you will need, but some states make a combined state law poster available. Read the posters to familiarize yourself with **labor law requirements** and the various agencies that might conduct surprise visits.

Typical state **labor laws** to learn about include:

- Federal and state minimum wage laws, which include overtime rules, hiring youth under age 18, and pay stub rules
- Employee classification and workers compensation insurance mandatory coverage
- Whether your state is a closed union shop state or a Right-

to-Work state, and if your legislature has modified the Common Law doctrine of Employment at Will which lets you fire bad employees whenever you want for any reason. If your state no longer permits this you will need to find out what procedures and documentation is involved to fire a poorly performing employee.
- OSHA unsafe work environment regulations
- Testing for drugs or other testing
- Time off for National Guard and other military duties as well as jury duty
- Discrimination complaints by employees or ex-employees to the federal or state **Equal Employment Opportunity Commission (EEOC)** and similar agencies

Many states offer free copies of required labor law posters on their Labor Department websites.

Federal labor law covers many more topics and the posters are harder to find. Start with the federal website page located at www.dol.gov/general/topics/posters to become familiar with these federal requirements. They include:

- **Fair Labor Standards Act** on minimum wage rates and when to pay employees
- Job Safety & Health (OSHA)
- **Family & Medical Leave Act** (which most startup businesses are exempt due to hiring less than 50 employees)
- **EEOC-related laws** on minorities, seasonal workers, disabled workers, and other similar special accommodation

required
- **Employee Polygraph Protection Act** if you test employees (such as for positions involving the handling of money)

If you contract to sell anything to the federal government there are additional laws you must comply with.

This long list of labor law and safety law requirements probably looks intimidating at first glance. However, most business owners find the impact is minimal on a daily basis until you grow to a level where you have over 50 employees or contract with the federal government.

Optional Filings

A final regulatory area for your business to consider is **optional filings** to protect intellectual property. This includes filing with your county clerk or Secretary of State to reserve a trade name. It can also include filing with the federal Patent Office for a patent, trademark, copyright, or other reservation service offered by this office. These government offices will not enforce your rights, but filing to reserve these intellectual property assets will strengthen any lawsuit you might consider initiating against a competitor infringing on your rights.

Tax planning and compliance can be very difficult and time-consuming. This is an area where an experienced CPA can guide you to minimize taxes and assure you keep up with the many tax and regulatory filing requirements throughout the year. You do not need to know all the details of these many, ever-changing laws. You just have to understand the basics enough to avoid major pitfalls and to know the right kinds of questions to ask your CPA.

22

Financing Options

Very few businesses can operate without borrowings of some sort. Initially, you will deposit some of your personal savings as startup capital into the business checking account to get things moving. From there, the business can consider a variety of financing sources. Each has its advantages and disadvantages, and some of them may not be open to your business, or the company might never grow to a point where you need to utilize some of them.

During the first few years, many entrepreneurs rely upon lending their savings to the new company, using personal credit cards for business expenses, drawing down a home line of credit, or taking a loan from a retirement plan. Banks typically shy away from lending to new startups because of the high uncertainty of repayment. However, leasing companies are more willing to take a risk on financing equipment and furnishings for your new company.

Creative Financing

During the early years as they build a customer base, entrepreneurs often look for creative financing. For example, you can offer a small **discount** if customers pay quickly, or **accept credit cards** to speed cash inflow. Coupled with that, try to negotiate 30 or 45 day **payment terms** with key suppliers to slow outflow. This helps you cover expenses that cannot be delayed, such as rent, taxes, and employee wages. Some suppliers may offer floor financing or consignment shipments of your inventory, allowing you a brief time to sell and collect from customers before you need to pay your vendors for the product purchased and sold first. Don't overlook financing from **customers**. The company might offer customers a discount for a substantial advance deposit towards the purchase of a higher-priced item.

If you still find yourself in a cash crunch during the early years, consider **factoring**. Factors will pay you upfront as soon as you present a signed sales contract, and not be as concerned about your new company's lack of credit rating. The factor will then take over the chore of pursuing the collection of the account receivable. There are two types of factoring. The first is **recourse factoring**. Recourse means if your customer does not pay the sales contract in full your firm is obligated to make up the difference. Recourse factoring involves a lower discount off the face value of the receivable (less costly for you). The second is **non-recourse factoring**. Non-recourse means if the factoring company cannot collect in full from your customer then your business is not liable for the difference. Of course, this higher risk for the factoring company comes with greater scrutiny of your customer quality and higher factoring discounts, resulting in your business receiving a lower percentage of the receivable from the factor. Factoring is more expensive than bank loans but it can be a viable alternative for a young business that has not yet built up a track record with a bank.

Lending Companies

After the first few years, particularly after the five-year mark, companies growing rapidly often see new sources of funding appear. An increasingly popular source of funds can be private non-bank lending companies. They offer loans similar to banks but do not take depository accounts such as checking and savings as a full bank would. Both bank and non-bank lenders will focus on several key credit factors:

- Ability to repay (the free cash flow generated compared to loan payments)
- Willingness to repay (assumed to be reflected in your credit score and repayment history on previous loans)
- Lender protection (liquidation value of assets to cover repayment of the loan if you default or get behind on payments)

If you form a corporation or LLC for liability protection purposes do not be surprised if the bank or lending company requires you to personally guarantee the loan with your personal assets (house, savings, car, etc.). This is a typical condition for most small businesses until the business has built a ten-year or more track record of paying all loans in full and is not under-capitalized. Low capitalization, usually reflected in a debt to equity ratio greater than 1.0:1, can not only make lenders nervous, some states have insolvency laws from the early 1800s allowing any petitioner to ask a court for a takeover of your company if net stockholder equity is negative. This type of law is considered complementary to federal bankruptcy law, but the few states that still have insolvency laws provide less protection than federal bankruptcy law.

Personal loans to a company from the entrepreneur are common to float temporary dips in cash flow or an uncommon need for a large amount of cash, such as the purchase of an expensive piece of equipment. Tax laws require the company to pay or accrue taxable interest to the shareholder each year and to properly document the loan in the company's board minutes. Lenders will also require any shareholder loans to be subordinated in priority to the bank's or lender's higher repayment and asset security.

Financing Stages

New companies that grow into larger companies rapidly (typically within a decade or so) progress through a series of financing stages. The **seed stage** is nearly always funded by the entrepreneur's savings and personal borrowing ability.

Moving into the **incubator stage** (whether housed in a formal business incubator or not) entrepreneurial companies look to family and friends for a small amount of **capital infusion** combined with creative financing techniques to utilize supplier and customer financing, as described earlier.

Later stages of growth fund rapid expansion that moves faster than revenue and cash collections, which will often lead to **angel investors** and a bit later **venture capital firms**. After that more rapid continued expansion, which continues to burn cash, may require what are referred to as "A" and "B" rounds of larger financing packages that require **Securities and Exchange Commission (SEC) regulatory filings**. After that many companies experiencing **hypergrowth** (a term loosely defined as a steep growth in sales averaging a minimum of 40% annually) may need more capital infusion. Closely related to this is the term **burn rate** which is defined as the rate in the number of months of accelerated performance projected to reach a cash flow break-even situation where the revenue collected can pay all the bills without seeking more capital infusions or loan proceeds.

Government Programs

Smaller, modest growth companies that have trouble attracting bank financing have some government programs available for help, although these come at a cost. Contrary to myth, there are no government grants of "free money" for small businesses, with the lone exception of **Small Business

Technology Development research grants to patent and develop new high-tech products. Even these grants, capped at $50,000, require the company to invest far more over several years before possibly qualifying for such a grant, and receiving the grant is unlikely for the majority of small businesses.

The **United States Small Business Administration (SBA)** will assist small firms by guaranteeing private bank loans as an incentive for a bank to lend to your company with reduced risk exposure for the bank. Your personal risk exposure on everything you own as well as all of your company assets is typically the price of obtaining an SBA loan guarantee, and interest rates are usually higher than normal bank loans. The bank will need to apply for the SBA guarantee, but you will fill out many government application forms and financial statements to provide to the bank.

The most common types of **SBA loan guarantees** are:

- **7(a) loans** – used for working capital up to $5 million, or purchasing equipment and other fixed assets. These are typically term loans (monthly repayments required)
- **CDC/504 loans** – to purchase commercial real estate (a mortgage)
- **CAPLines** – government-guaranteed portion of a line of credit
- **Export loans** – to finance product sales to international customers
- **Microloans** – small working capital loans up to a maximum of $50,000

- **Disaster loans** – available only in a declared national natural disaster area, to existing small businesses, and with additional **Federal Emergency Disaster Administration (FEMA)** paperwork and approvals

Many small business owners feel the extra time, paperwork requirements, higher interest rates, and personal risk exposure are not worth the effort to attempt obtaining an SBA loan. However, rapidly growing companies may find their banks require the SBA loan to become comfortable enough to lend to your company.

If your company is growing rapidly, state and local governments have programs that provide other forms of **partial financing**. A common one is offered by state unemployment offices. If you agree to hire at least 15 to 50 new employees (the exact number varies by state) at that state's minimum wage level or higher, and provide health insurance, the state will conduct training programs at taxpayer expense. Additionally, it might agree to offer a subsidy or discount on state taxes for the first 90 days of new worker employment.

Larger companies can occasionally command cash incentives from local governments, but small businesses rarely have that much leverage. Yet you might obtain tax incentives (exemption from one or more types of taxes for a few years) if you hire at least 50 employees with an agreed-upon minimum level of wages plus health insurance, within a limited period of time.

In addition, if you are building a factory all states administer a federal program called **Community Block Development Grants (CBDG)**. These are grants to a local government or a special kind of nonprofit usually controlled by a local government to subsidize new roads, sewer and water lines, and other infrastructure improvements to an industrial park site where you plan to build. Sometimes local governments will even build the building and rent it to you at a favorable rate for a fixed number of years to help your company establish productivity in their community.

Of course, these incentives also come with a similar requirement to provide a certain number of well-paying jobs with benefits that will generate enough tax revenue to offset the benefit offered to your company. But this can be a good form of financing if your company is growing rapidly enough to qualify.

As high-growth companies approach break even on the burn rate their founders will take one of two approaches. Selling the company to a larger company allows early investors and the entrepreneur to cash out, and simultaneously provides a richer source of capital to continue growing the company.

Selling Stock

The other approach is to make a private stock sale to an investment banking firm in what is called **mezzanine** or **bridge financing** for a short time to pay for the expensive and time-consuming cost of making an **Initial Public Offering (IPO)** to sell stock to the general public.

This second approach is often coupled with the stock becoming listed either over-the-counter or on a stock exchange, bringing in more capital and public accountability while allowing the entrepreneur to liquidate and cash in on those hard years of lean efforts while still maintaining control over the company. The big drawback to going public is far greater government cost and scrutiny for regulatory filings and pressure from stock analysts and the general public for short term stock price gains at the possible expense of longer-term strategic moves, as well as giving up some of your ownership to obtain capital instead of borrowing.

If you decide to pursue additional capital infusions the following is a quick summary of the key provisions for each of the three smaller business federal securities regulations filings.

Regulations

	A+	D	Crowdfunding
Offering Maximum Size	Tier 1 $20M Tier 2 $50M	$5M	
Prospectus Type	Offering Circular	Form D or private memorandum	Form C
Financial Statements Requirements	Semi-annual Audited	Annual audited	< $100K: raised executive officer certification > $100K: CPA annual reviewed
Advertising & Solicitation	Circular only, either online or paper	Accredited investors only	Websites of Broker-Dealers or Funding Portals
Investor Qualifications	Tier 1: anyone Tier 2: accredited investors only	Accredited investors only	Anyone

The more money you want to raise the more expensive and strict the filing requirements. Plus, the more selective the potential investors you may talk to. The main requirement to observe is whether you must restrict information to accredited investors only. The SEC definition of an Accredited Investor is someone with a net value of investments and savings (excluding house, car, etc.) above $1 million (or someone who earns more than $200,000 per year).

Note the far lower and less onerous registration requirements to offer stock under the relatively new Crowdfunding regulation. You can raise anywhere from $100,000 to $1,000,000 by publicizing your offering over SEC-approved Broker-Dealer or Funding Portal websites to anyone in any state. This dollar range overlaps with the typical small business bank loan range.

This is the federal government's requirement. Each state also has securities filing requirements. State laws are traditionally referred to as **Blue Sky** laws. In addition to filing under a federal securities regulation, you will also need to file a security offering registration and regular ongoing reports in each state where you solicit investors, whether or not anyone in that state purchases your stock or not. In addition to these interstate requirements, each state also has intra-state regulations. The difference is for an intrastate offering both the company and the investors must all reside within the same state. If you meet this requirement and limit your offering solely to other residents in your state then you are exempt from federal filing requirements, since the offering does not cross a state boundary. State Blue Sky laws can vary widely.

For example, in my home state of North Carolina, a company may offer up to $2 million in securities (either stocks or bonds) using the state Blue Sky form and providing quarterly audited or reviewed financial statements (your choice). You may offer these securities only through a Broker-Dealer registered with the state as an intrastate website. Investors, whether accredited or not, may not purchase more than $5,000 of your securities during a 12 month period. This is a fairly typical type of intrastate Blue Sky crowdfunding law, although requirements vary widely from state to state. If you wish to pursue any registered or exempt securities offerings, even a very small one, you should consult an attorney who is experienced in such registrations.

Unique Challenges of Nonprofits and Charitable Organizations

At this point, let us pivot to the unique challenges if you started a **nonprofit** or **charitable organization** rather than a for-profit business. Many of the financing alternatives discussed in this chapter would be closed to you. There are no investors in a nonprofit because there are no owners or stockholders. Likewise, the SBA will not lend to you, nor can you raise capital because you have no return on investment you may offer.

However, a nonprofit corporation can still utilize several creative financing techniques. If you charge a fee for a product or service the cash flow management techniques discussed in this chapter are still available for you to apply. Likewise, a business operated as either a part of the nonprofit mission or as a for-profit subsidiary owned by the nonprofit might qualify for bank financing.

Local governments are sometimes willing to sell and finance charities buildings they are no longer using at favorable terms. In turn, your nonprofit might cover the loan or lease payments by subleasing to other nonprofits with complementary missions that can create a synergistic benefit for a group of charities in the community. As the building manager, an entrepreneur might also negotiate subsidies from the other building tenants to fund a receptionist, utilities, and other overhead for all building occupants, thus reducing your labor and administrative costs.

Grant-makers prefer to look for leverage, as well as significant community service improvements. Taking the building example, if you gathered a consortium of charities into the building your nonprofit is purchasing, you might be more likely to obtain a grant to help cover operating costs. Large foundations might also be more willing to consider **capacity building grants** when you present a synergistic group of charities working together under your roof.

Don't overlook the value of volunteers. They cut your labor costs substantially. An increasing number of cities have volunteer centers to help you recruit volunteers, and community foundations to help connect with potential donors.

Nonprofit corporations can still sell products and services without limitation. If what you are selling is unrelated to the charitable mission of your organization then you will pay a type of income tax on that income (but not donations or investment income). This type of tax is called an **Unrelated Business Taxable Income (UBTI) tax**.

However, if you can tie in business operations to the charitable mission then there would be no UBTI tax, although you will still have a sales tax, payroll taxes, and other types of taxation. An example would be Goodwill Industries stores which receive donated discarded goods for sale then sell them at steeply discounted prices. Profits are utilized to train poorer residents with job skills that will qualify them for better-paying jobs with local businesses, which is a large part of Goodwill's mission, as well as a self-funding business mechanism not reliant on cash donations. Upon applying some entrepreneurial creativity the possibilities for creating tax-free revenue streams is nearly endless.

Nonprofits have a particularly creative long-term financing tool available which a small but growing number of charities are beginning to exploit. Affluent donors who want to help support your mission can make major donations at very little cost with a charitable remainder trust. An irrevocable trust is set up, holding a large life insurance policy as its sole asset, based upon the life of a donor in the 75 to 85 age range in moderate health. The beneficiary is the trust. A participating bank will lend money to pay the premiums with the expectation that the loan and interest will be paid from the insurance proceeds upon death, and the balance of funds remaining will be disbursed to the charity. In most states, the donor must pay a small one-time fee of a few hundred dollars to initiate a multi-million dollar policy. This financing technique does not create funding in the short term, but over a decade or more it can build many millions of dollars towards accomplishing your charity's mission at very little cost to either the charity or your generous donors.

V

Cross-Cultural Leadership

This section covers how you can build leadership skills in other people connected to your company.

Chapter 23 examines how you can intentionally create goals and culture to reflect your interests.

Chapter 24 explores principles and theories for developing motivated and focused employees.

Chapter 25 examines the fuzzy line between employees and vendors in many entrepreneurial organizations.

Chapter 26 teaches you how to actively and regularly pursue self-improvement.

23

Building Corporate Culture & Goal Setting

Culture can be viewed from various perspectives. Let us start with the big picture of national or regional cultures, drilling down into the organizational culture you are trying to develop. National culture reflects how most people in a particular country tend to view the reality and behavior around them.

National Culture

Professor Geert Hofstede defined six general or broad dimensions of **national culture**. They are:

Power Distance – relationship power recognition in societal institutions such as employers, family, and other social organizations between leaders and group members. An example would be how comfortable or acceptable it might be to offer suggestions or criticisms of leadership ideas and how familiar versus formal or distant a member and leader might be in talking with one another

Individualism – the extent to which people feel independent or free to make their own choices alone or with minimal consultation or approval from others versus a collectivist concept where people feel more comfortable fitting within a well-defined place in life determined by social interactions and relationships around them ("knowing one's place").

Masculinity – this is a behavioral reaction in which societies that lean towards masculine expression on this scale tend to use authority or force interactions between people versus the femininity end of the scale where emotional closeness and sympathy for others' situations is valued more highly. This is not a male or female perspective; it is more about the level of emphasis on emotional intelligence versus relying more heavily upon intellectual and authority arguments during discussions and interactions

Uncertainty Avoidance – measurement of how uncomfortable (such as anxious or distrustful or wary) people feel with unknown circumstances, resulting in a desire to follow predefined habits and behavioral rules in an attempt to know or control the truth and their environment versus embracing uncertainty without much concern or looking forward to learning and experiencing new things

Long Term Orientation – within this dimension people look to change the future over time because they view the world as continually modifying and can be improved, versus the other extreme of this scale where people think mostly in short term periods and see little to no change expected and the current status quo is assumed to be generally a morally good one (or at least as good as it can get)

Indulgence – an indulgent lifestyle views doing whatever you want whenever you want and enjoying relationships with others as the greatest good. The other end of this scale can be called a "restrained culture" in which life is typically assumed to be difficult and duty is the norm rather than anticipating much personal freedom

If you conduct business in more than one nation or sometimes see regional variances within a nation, these dimensions can help you understand what to expect and how you might need to modify your company operations. For example, one entrepreneur I know has operations in both a Muslim Middle Eastern nation and the United States. The American employees are eager to express their ideas for improving operations (low Power Distance) and will seek opportunities to solve customer problems (high Individualism and somewhat high Masculinity). They tend not to feel much concern or doubt over their ability to fix operational challenges when problems occur (low Uncertainty Avoidance) and think about short-term goals while considering longer-term company potential advancements (moderate level of Long Term Orientation). American employees at this company also expect employee benefit plans and request vacation time off, family time accommodations, and other similar perks (high Indulgence scores).

In contrast, the Middle Eastern office employees will wait until receiving specific instructions on how to resolve specific problems (very high Power Distance, low Individualism, and high Masculinity scores). The manager's opinions are highly respected, and he is assumed to know more about how operations should be run than any employees. Company rules and training are important to these employees, as well as complying with government and company paperwork requirements. They obediently follow procedural steps even if the reason for such actions or forms is not clearly evident to the employee and they are slow to accept changes in corporate procedures (very high Uncertainty Avoidance). Employees assume the current compensation and job requirements are fair and should remain so (low Long Term Orientation and low Indulgence scores).

Coordination between these two offices is sometimes difficult due to these cultural differences in employee attitudes. Neither is better or worse than the other, just different. Managers must show more initiative and attention to detail on everything in the Middle Eastern office, but this fits the culture and business climate in that area. Managers in the USA office can test new ideas more easily in the American office before exporting organizational procedural changes to the other office, but the bulk of production occurs more smoothly and at a lower cost in the Middle Eastern office. Of course, these national cultural differences also require different approaches to sharing Biblical insights with employees, customers, and vendors in each location, just as the apostle Paul used different approaches with the Jews than when talking with Greeks.

Organizational Culture

Another outlook on culture is organizational culture promoted within your company. There are another six commonly considered dimensions to organizational culture. Briefly, they are:

Means versus Goal Oriented – this scores the amount of emphasis on how (means) versus what (goals) is accomplished. Another way to consider this dimension is avoiding risk through preferring processes rather than achieving an end which tends to result in greater organizational effectiveness but with higher variance or risk in results

Internally or Externally Driven – internally focused employees consider themselves experts offering what they know customers should want. Externally oriented employees ask customers what they want and pursue those customer desires

Easygoing versus Strict Discipline – an informal and often unpredictable work environment often encourages innovation. The other end of this spectrum insists upon extensive planning and efficient productivity

Local versus Professional – locally-oriented employees identify primarily with their close coworkers and tend towards low-diversity groupthink. Profession-oriented employees tend to identify more with their profession or occupation and type of work rather than their own team

Open or Closed System – this dimension measures levels of quick acceptance of a new employee as compared to the level of requirement for newcomers to prove themselves and earn acceptance

Employee-Centered versus Work-Centered – leaders in employee-centered organizations promote employee satisfaction, even if it costs some productivity. Work-centered leaders pursue goals and high accomplishment regardless of the impact on employees

Obviously, extremes can be harmful to the sustainability of any organization over more than a brief period. However, the majority of companies fall somewhere between extremes on each organizational dimension. Neither pole of each dimension are good or bad, simply different.

Having defined cultural dimensions for both national or regional areas as well as company cultural dimensions within an organization, you should be able to recognize areas of potential misunderstanding and aspects of your employees' attitudes that you as the entrepreneurial founder might need to work on changing, or at least adjusting your leadership style to improve your effectiveness across differing cultures your company operates within.

Motivation

Building an organizational culture depends upon the **consensus** you promote and reinforce with **incentives**. Some companies list attributes or attitudes all employees should exhibit. But that requires example and reinforcement from leadership (you), which we will discuss in chapter twenty. Incentives and disincentives, both monetary compensation and recognition in front of peers, should consistently promote **company values**.

From where is **motivation** derived? For many non-Christians, the higher purpose they pursue is a humanistic desire for self-actualization. They find meaning in the work itself, or from the job position's status, rewards, and recognition. Inevitably you will hire some people who pursue this type of motivation. *Over the longer term, this basis of motivation leads to burnout and disillusionment, since no earthly goal can fully satisfy the inherent image of God within each of us.*

A Biblical perspective still requires "our daily bread" to survive, and personal recognition motivates people, but Christians respond from a deeper basis. Responding to God's love should be the basis for all that Christians accomplish in life, whether expressed in the many work hours invested to help others as we support ourselves, or in worship or among our family relations, charitable efforts in the community, and other aspects of our life. Lasting satisfaction comes from God alone, through or using work and other aspects of our life, not from "uplifting" or helpful work itself. This is perhaps a very difficult motivational base to instill among non-

Christian coworkers, although most will respond positively when surrounded by a Biblically-informed consensus.

Reaching across cultural boundaries and motivating employees to pursue company goals requires instilling and reinforcing your company values. Employees will respond from either an **intrinsic** or **extrinsic motivation**. This means the employee is motivated by either self-motivation (intrinsic desire to achieve company and personal goals) or via external forces. Either way, you customize incentives for the employee's motivational orientation. A Christian employer should encourage an organizational culture that conveys a feeling of making a difference for others and caring for both employees and customers.

To reinforce this, managers should celebrate little things and progress towards goals. Biblically-based businesses can encourage employees to see the business as a starting point extending out into charity work and other involvement towards improving the community. Entrepreneurs can lead by example while also providing support and resources. An example would be the Chick-Fil-A franchisees who give free food and drinks during local disasters and even to protesters picketing their restaurants, showing compassion to those opposed to a Christian business witness. Employees receive not only training for polite and caring responses to all customers and community members, but they also see the franchise owner modeling these values.

If you need to change your corporate culture, how is that accomplished? The steps involved include framing the issue or cultural aspect needing change. Demonstrate and celebrate quick wins, even if small at first. Build coalitions to form larger networks of support for change. Create safe havens where risk and some failure are tolerated in order to promote experimentation. Embrace symbols or create cultural artifacts (tee shirts, buttons, office parties, awards, etc.) that reinforce the desired behavior and direction. Finally, remove financial and other incentives that support the undesired behavior you are trying to change. Above all, be patient. You are dealing with human beings. Accept that making small, incremental changes takes time.

Initially, you probably want to focus on small group modeling of change if you have grown to a moderate-sized business. If you are still small enough that your employees constitute a small group then you should work at change on a one-on-one basis.

The **Group Stages of Development Theory,** first proposed by Bruce Tuckman in 1965, involves the following steps:

Forming – This step involves picking a team that you think can work together, identifying team goals, and encouraging them to get to know each other and openly share with one another freely without personal criticism of individuals. Promote only open questioning of ideas.

Storming – Often thought of as the creative step, storming should encourage wide-open sharing of ideas. How practical and affordable each idea might be can be sorted later. During this step of the process, the team should build an inventory of potential ideas to explore later.

Norming – During the norming stage, all the ideas are analyzed from a variety of viewpoints among the team members to resolve conflicting suggestions, and determine the most efficient and effective approach towards achieving the team's goals.

Performing – Once the team comes together in a common agreement on the course of action to pursue, the next obvious action is to implement the new chosen idea and monitor initial performance to assure both success and sustainability.

Adjourning – In this final step the team may be disbanded to participate in other projects, or if you are still in the very small startup stage of your company growth you might provide additional goals for the team to pursue. An important part of this adjourning stage is taking some time to celebrate the team's success. This builds confidence in each team member, encourages future innovation and willingness to share new ideas, and reinforces their ability to successfully accept and implement improvements.

Setting Goals

In this chapter on building company culture and goal setting, we have not yet covered the question of setting goals. Obviously, this book cannot anticipate the ever-evolving company needs you may face at the moment and suggest specific goals for you. But we can discuss overarching approaches to goal setting. Longer-term or bigger goals and their subset, shorter and smaller objectives, should be specific, measurable, attainable, action-oriented, and have a set time frame for accomplishment.

To help motivate staff, write or post the company goals and progress achieved towards those goals, especially shorter-term progress. Try to stick with no more than three goals at a time, and prioritize if you run into time or resource conflicts, so employees will have a clear understanding of what is most important to you.

The Bible has many passages providing guidance on goals and implementation. Most of this advice concerns what is typically considered the area of ethics or how we implement goals and the type of goals pursued. Keep in mind these boundaries. Chasing the highest return on investment might seem acceptable but such a mindset can frequently lead to unrighteous behavior and thinking. Sometimes it is best to give up some profit or accept an unjust result (such as refunding revenue to a customer who abused your product or did not follow the advice you provided).

What are common Biblical parameters for goal setting? The most helpful approach to reading all of God's guidance is to read a portion of the Bible daily. For now, the following is a brief sample list, although by no means an exhaustive one:

Compensation - (Proverbs 10:16) The wage of the righteous leads to life, the gain of the wicked to sin. (This applies to you as an entrepreneur, your company's business conduct, and how you compensate both employees and vendors).

Clarity – (Genesis 2:15 & Genesis 3:23) Cultivate and guard or preserve (*Shamar*) the earth, including celebrating God's gifts to us and allowing both people and creation a regular time for refreshment, renewal, and honoring the Creator (Exodus 20:8-11). Over-working for long periods leads to burnout, increasing mistakes, resentment, and other harms to individuals and the company. Life balance is a Biblical principle, as is rest.

Calling – (Ephesians 2:10) For we are His workmanship, created in Christ Jesus for good works, which God prepared beforehand, that we should walk in them. This includes both paid and volunteer service.

Attitude of Justice – (Colossians 3:17-4:1) We are called to give thanks in all relationships, including those of employers, employees, spouses, parents, and to be fair and just in our daily dealings with one another.

Skills – (Proverbs 22:29) Each of us is to apply our skills to the glory of God, not concerned about the recognition from others that will naturally come without our need to boast or promote ourselves.

Influence – (Titus 2) We are to call out those in senior positions to set good examples in their actions and words. What about verses 9 and 10 that speak to "bondslaves" or employees? The very first opening introduction to Titus from Paul, who is a widely acknowledged leader in the church, shows Paul self-identifying as himself a "bondslave" to Jesus. We all fit into a hierarchy, including entrepreneurs, and will be held accountable for whatever level or amount of influence we have on others by our example, words, and station in life. Matthew 5:16 summarizes this for both entrepreneurs and your employees to "let your light shine before others, so that they may see your good works and give glory to your Father who is in heaven." Since we spend the majority of our waking time at work or conducting transactions, the marketplace portion of our lives provides a powerful opportunity to express the impact Jesus can make.

Relationships – (Hebrews 3:13) The Bible urges us to place encouragement and honesty first in our dealings with others. The book of James is frequently misunderstood. It does not say you can be saved through any works of your own but does express multiple times that the joy of salvation should be reflected to others through your response to God in all you do, including your company. Christian businesses provide temporal help for earthly needs, as called for in James 2:15-17, both to help fellow humans and as a response to what God is doing for us. Christian entrepreneurs can utilize that starting point of meeting others' temporal needs to gain permission for discussing a more lasting, eternal solution for the God-shaped need in each person's heart. Also, following this Biblical guidance helps navigate workplace challenges and tends to develop healthier relationships.

When setting business goals, this ethical framework can help you and those associated with you—both employees and vendors—from losing sight of the most productive and effective ways to further both your company and God's goals in the marketplace. A Biblical framework can also guide you on how to correct faulty thinking or actions, and when to terminate an employee or vendor relationship that runs counter to the culture and community witness you are striving to present.

24

Employee Development

Setting goals and objectives for employees, while providing incentives and penalties to assure high-quality performance, are certainly important elements of managing employees. But truly leading your employees involves much more effort on your part. There are many academic theories on leadership and even a few on followership. You may identify with or feel most comfortable expressing your leadership to employees through one of the six most commonly cited leadership styles, depending on your personality and temperament.

Those leadership approaches are:

- **Transactional**—use "carrot and stick" approach of contingent rewards and "management by exception" corrections to offer exchanges of results for rewards
- **Charismatic**—inspiring and expecting employees to achieve high performance based on strongly believed core values, vision conveyed, leader self-sacrifice, decisive actions, trustworthiness, and high-performance

orientation. Charismatic leaders utilize emotional intelligence to galvanize employees towards giving their best effort always
- **Transformational**—provides idealized influence about desired attitudes, behaviors, and performance as well as inspirational motivation and intellectual stimulation for job enrichment, all provided by the leader as individualized consideration for which particular rewards motivate each worker
- **Authentic**—transmit genuine, trustworthy, and ethically grounded leadership that is transparent and responsive to other people's needs and values, emphasizing self-awareness based upon critical life events
- **Servant**—focuses on leader behaviors consisting of conceptualizing desired results for each follower, emotional healing and encouragement, supporting employees first before leadership, helping employees grow and succeed in their jobs, stressing ethical behavior, urging empowerment and creating value for the community (defined as customers then spreading outward to others). This type of leader pictures company structure as an upside-down pyramid, with the leader at the bottom motivating employees to desire doing likewise in pleasing customers at the top of the pyramid. An old Roman Catholic leadership saying summarizes this concept: "The Pope is the servant of the servants of God"

While Christians may instinctively gravitate towards trying to model servant leadership as the leadership style that most seems to fit Jesus' leadership, there are advantages and disadvantages to each leadership approach, including servant leadership. This is inherent because all leaders are also sinful humans bearing both the glory of being made in God's image, as well as the brokenness of inheriting and compounding original sin. Each person is also unique in God's eye, so no single leadership style fits every leader, just as no single template for employee motivation fits all workers' personalities.

Smaller, entrepreneurial firms grow faster when the leader hires, trains, and motivates employees to show creativity and self-initiative. This involves ensuring employees that they have more flexibility to take risks, even though that may cost you more in the short term. Employees frequently value such flexibility as additional motivation, feeling you value them as important team members allowed to make some decisions. Of course, this must be tempered with their experience and level of expertise, since a major costly mistake by an employee could destroy a small company. However, many employees rise to meet your expectations when they feel the opportunity to contribute significantly towards company success.

Employee leadership starts with carefully considering which job candidates to hire. It is very difficult to determine ahead of time which ones will prove successful employees. Once hired the entrepreneur should provide training on what is expected. This involves expectations for the particular job and how that job contributes to overall company productivity. Also, explain company values and goals, and spend time monitoring the new employee for the first few months. Most businesses find that it takes between six months to a year before the company begins earning a profit from new employee labor.

Offering Benefits and Incentives

Smaller, entrepreneurial companies can often compete on wages, but have difficulty matching fringe benefit plans than larger, more established competitors offer. You can appear more attractive than the larger company if you concentrate on the small firm's non-financial enhancements, which larger corporations usually cannot afford.

These advantages include greater flexibility for personal time off, holidays, company picnics, or other fun family events, the opportunity for more responsibility, learning new skills, and creating growth possibilities for the company along with extra compensation as the company increases its revenue from the employee's efforts. That lack of bureaucratic format can make the smaller company seem more enjoyable. Greater flexibility is very attractive, especially for part-time employees. Stronger personal relationships among a close-knit team also make working for a smaller company often more enjoyable.

There are still many financial benefit plans you can offer too. Most brokerage firms, banks, and insurance companies now provide tax-saving small business retirement plans for no administrative fees, costing your company nothing to offer this employee perk. When you can afford it you might consider matching employee contributions up to a reasonable amount. Small business associations and local Chamber of Commerce organizations typically have discounted benefits plans for vision, dental, legal services, and similar items which you can offer at little to no cost to your company as payroll deductions, sometimes on a pre-tax saving basis.

Medical coverage is a major concern for Americans. There is a tax credit for smaller companies sponsoring health insurance. But even after the credit, the cost tends to remain unaffordable for most small business owners. You still have an alternative. You can sponsor a tax-advantaged **Health Savings Account (HSA)** or **Flexible Spending Account (FSA)** combined with a high deductible health insurance plan where the employee pays a large portion of the premium via payroll deduction. Another possibility is providing **Medical Reimbursement Plans** which are a tax deduction for your company while remaining tax-free to employees. Each of these options allows you to provide some form of medical coverage while letting you control the cost so the expenditures do not crush your startup firm. A similar arrangement applies to dependent care, which can be combined with flexible work hours to accommodate your employees' child care situations.

If you expand into hiring employees or contractors in other nations, entrepreneurial companies can offer unique incentives. These might include a trip to the United States after several years of working for the company or simply sending Christmas presents or cash bonuses to international employees, who are frequently paid far less than Americans and lack nearly all the fringe benefit plans of their American counterparts. These smaller, more affordable incentives boost morale and motivation substantially.

Another area where entrepreneurs can boost productivity with incentives is by tying company prosperity or lean times directly to revenue, helping employees understand that sales are the source of their compensation. Most employees have trouble understanding or feeling any urgency about building company profitability. However, if you offer both short and longer-term bonuses tied to increased profitability employees will eventually catch on. In smaller firms, it is easier to customize incentives to each employee's particular job and individual initiative or productivity, since there are fewer governmental labor regulations imposed to restrict your creativity until you reach fifty employees.

Because smaller companies tend to have stronger, closer relationships between employees and more informal interaction with the business owner it may be easier for you to try efficiency improvements, such as a Kaizen event. The Kaizen event, developed in Japan, involves closing company operations for a day while carefully walking through each action, paperwork form, and staff position to determine which aspects slow production or are unnecessary. Kaizen events have proven to substantially improve speed, cost savings, and overall efficiency and responsiveness. But they will scare employees concerned about losing their jobs unless you state a commitment to retain them and reposition each redundant employee into expanding the company's output instead.

Of course, there is a point where a few employees fail to respond to corrections or create morale problems among other employees, and the only solution is to terminate their employment. Dr. Jim Collins developed what he calls the

Hedgehog Theory. The core thought in this theory is to get the right people in the right seats, realigning assignments, and providing training coupled with appropriate incentives. But sometimes there is no right seat for a few people who resist needed change, so those employees must be taken off the bus entirely for the company to pick up speed towards reaching its goals.

Spiritual Support and Outreach

As Christian entrepreneurs, we can also provide a spiritual dimension to the workplace. Some midsized companies contract for a corporate chaplain service. There are several such companies providing chaplains to assist employees with personal counseling and a Biblical perspective on life issues. Smaller firms sometimes sponsor employee Bible studies or prayer sessions at work.

The employer/employee relationship will naturally limit the level of openness in such discussions, but some discussion is definitely possible, particularly along the lines of how company personnel can convey a righteous witness to vendors, customers, non-Christian employees, and the community. Contrary to what some non-Christian activists claim, such spiritual efforts in the workplace are not illegal, and are included in your and your employees' First Amendment rights for freedom of religion and free speech, as recognized by the United States Supreme Court.

If correction is needed, always provide discipline in private.

A correlating idea is to praise in public, which encourages both the employee and his or her peers to perform better. Document problem issues in each employee's personnel file. Most states still support the "at-will" legal doctrine that the employee serves "at the will and pleasure of the employer" and therefore no reason is needed to fire anyone. However, it is always prudent to maintain a historic trail of problems and the corrections applied, as not all states are as friendly to employers as "at-will" employment states.

From a Christian perspective, compassion and grace are appropriate, with the amount of grace offered gradually declining as an employee repeats persistent problem areas. When termination is required the Christian business owner should usually consider going beyond legal requirements (which are minimal) to offering help if you are aware that the employee's personal or family situation will be difficult if fired. Smaller businesses cannot afford to give large severances, but you might consider a small one, a good reference letter (if warranted), and referrals. One action you should not consider is leaving a problematic employee in the workplace to negatively influence fellow employees and customers, and in a few cases sabotage or steal company records. Eliminate this possibility with a quiet, swift termination.

Not all employee assistance can or should be known to others. I have seen Christian business owners quietly help individuals through a divorce, purchasing a car when an employee's finances are very low, and many other situations. Perhaps one of the most carefully thought out examples I witnessed was a client of mine who asked me to investigate possible embezzlement. I did indeed uncover the theft committed by his office manager. We talked and prayed over the godliest solution. Then he called the sheriff and district attorney, presented my evidence, and had the employee arrested.

When the ex-employee was released from prison the entrepreneur offered him a job, but not handling money anymore. The then convicted criminal accepted the job working on the loading dock since he could not find a job anywhere else. Yet the re-hired employee bitterly complained about the business owner to other employees. The entrepreneur continued to tolerate this situation for several years until the employee found a job elsewhere. The part of the story known only to me and my client is that during the employee's time in prison his family's living expenses and mortgage payment were secretly paid by the business owner, so his wife and children would not suffer from his moral failure, and to encourage the family to stay together.

This type of employee assistance can sometimes create loyalty and motivation from employees, but as in the example above, you should not count on that result. The reason to provide such assistance is that Christ calls us to care for others.

Christian entrepreneurs need not feel bad about poor hiring decisions or employees who fail to perform up to expected standards. Develop a compassionate transition for such employees within the limited resources available to you, such as some severance pay. Let them file for unemployment claims (which will cost you in higher state unemployment taxes for the next several years, so that higher tax rate must be factored into what you can afford), and offer a good reference when possible.

Nonprofits

Accountability is more difficult in a nonprofit situation where you have very little control over volunteers, unlike employees. Smaller startup nonprofits relying fully on volunteers or with only the Chief Executive Director (CEO) who might be paid. Motivation and quality control becomes a bit easier when there is a mix of volunteers and paid staff, including a paid coordinator of volunteers to track scheduling, training, and performance evaluation of each volunteer worker. For some types of nonprofits, such as churches and some charities, a bifurcated leadership structure may be most effective, where a volunteer board chairman or president can hold volunteers more accountable than a paid staff member such as a pastor.

When an organization is large enough to afford recognition items, these small items can generate motivation and discipline among volunteers. Examples include the tee shirts and discount coupons offered by Red Cross to blood donors and disaster relief workers, or the tee shirts and free concert admissions when representing Compassion International at events. Some nonprofit organizations will hold an annual membership or supporter banquet which serves multiple purposes. The banquet may meet a state law requirement for an annual membership meeting in conjunction with a fundraising event, plus recognition of volunteers contributing significant amounts of time to the organization. A few nonprofits tie several levels of membership to the level of volunteer commitment, offering voting rights to elect the board of trustees to the most committed class of volunteers.

Regardless of whether you can afford staff yet or not, the baseball league's model offers an excellent approach to developing knowledgeable, committed volunteers. The baseball league model can be applied to nonprofit volunteers in this manner. Entry-level volunteers can be given specific lower-level tasks to do, supervised by either a more experienced volunteer or an employee, similar to the baseball "A" level. The next higher level—"AA" could be promoting an experienced volunteer to a committee appointment while asking for a minimum amount of involvement in both committee research and organizational activities. The top minor league position—equivalent to baseballs' "AAA" league—is to promote the experienced volunteer to chair a committee and become an elected board member. Board members should be expected to contribute both time and money towards the cause. Volunteers finally reach the "Major League" by demonstrating expertise, experience, and a strong commitment to the organization. This is reflected in becoming elected as an officer of the board. Additional duties should include mentoring and promoting those volunteers who demonstrate the most competence and commitment to furthering the organization's mission.

25

Vendor Development

Startup companies often utilize suppliers as substitutes for employees. Vendors can sometimes provide ideas for improving products or streamlining operations. Vendors can provide flexible labor rather than employee costs that are fixed regardless of whether or not those employees are productive all the time. Suppliers and contract labor can sometimes be good partners for growing your business if you recognize the legal and competitive limitations.

If your vendors and employees will be sharing and jointly developing ideas, you must approach the situation carefully. Many businesses simply purchase products or contracts for certain labor expertise, which provides minimal innovation generation.

Keiretsu

At the other extreme is the **Keiretsu** concept. Japanese companies coordinate their pricing, creative product, service progress, and all other aspects of business operations closely in harmony. This lock-step approach includes all members of the Keiretsu group owning each other's stock and holding membership on each other's boards, including full integration of manufacturing chains (both vertical and horizontal) plus banks and government agencies such as the powerful **Ministry of International Trade and Industry (MITI)**. If the group suffers a slump in sales, the "cure" is for banks to convert loans into stock. This extremely close coordination of all vendors within the supply chain is illegal in the United States. South Korea utilizes a very similar concept called **Zaibatsu** (originally a Japanese term) or **Chaebol**.

Partnering

If American companies want to receive synergistic benefits from sharing a portion of information with suppliers, they need to pursue the middle ground of avoiding price collusion and restricting competition. This somewhat closer swapping of partial ideas while still protecting intellectual property is called **partnering** in America. Most companies (though not all) require **Non-Disclosure Agreements (NDA)**, particularly when dealing with contractors or consultants, to limit or prevent loss of intellectual property such as trade secrets. As a practical matter, supplier cooperation can present legal and risk management challenges, so you should impose limits on what and how much data can be shared, particularly customer information.

Integrating Vendors

Yet there are several ways to integrate vendor suggestions and coordination. One popular concept is **Just In Time inventory (JIT)**. Under this agreement, your company would concentrate its supply orders with a favored vendor in exchange for volume discount pricing and a requirement that the vendor delivers the product or parts only when needed. That shifts the inventory or carrying costs to your vendor. Suppliers generally do not agree to such arrangements unless your company represents a significant amount of their sales.

Remember **Buyer Power**? Another common approach is to share the cost of financing inventory, whether work in progress or finished goods. That can be done through consignment arrangements where the supplier does not bill your company until you sell the product or until some agreed-upon delay of 30, 60, or 90 days, allowing your sales staff to sell and collect prior to paying for the product, thus greatly improving cash flow and making company expansion much easier to finance.

If you build significant buyer power, be careful not to impoverish key suppliers or contractors. The Biblical principle of compensating workers fairly for their labor also applies to your vendors. If you demand too much, you may go bankrupt or lose the ability to supply the materials you need, at the price you desire.

Returning to the cooperation concept, larger companies have pushed smaller suppliers into registering for **International Organization for Standardization (ISO) certification**, which requires an operations audit similar to the Kaizen event described previously in this book. If done carefully, this can result in faster and possibly more cost-effective or cash flow-saving improvements. It is a type of partnering which is legally acceptable in the United States. Young companies rarely can force ISO certification on their suppliers, and you may find your company on the receiving end from a large customer. In lieu of pursuing ISO, informal chats between companies can build trust and save some money without straining relationships between companies and their owners.

Remember the discussion earlier in this book about **Porter's 5 Forces**? The Buyer Power and Seller Power could easily be reversed on you when considering suppliers. Preventing these types of powers from being used against your company's purchases is not as quickly resolved as when we discussed key customers. You want to minimize the risk of one or a few customers representing a large portion of sales and therefore to give your customer leverage over you.

For purchases, the answer is more complicated. Avoiding the concentration of company purchases from a key vendor is not very important for most expenditures, except for inventory purchases for critical parts or a key subcontractor who might be in a position to steal a significant amount of your customers. Most suppliers can be replaced swiftly and easily.

The counterargument to avoiding concentration in one or a few key suppliers is to gradually build confidence in a supplier's pricing, reliability, and ethical behavior. Concentrating purchases, particularly inventory, with one or two suppliers provides tangible benefits such as pricing and payment terms breaks. It also provides intangible benefits such as obtaining quick turnarounds in emergencies or advice on product improvement since your supplier also sees your competitors improved products. In other words, it can be a fuzzy line between supplier loyalty versus a hostage situation.

As the company grows, consider gradually changing the mix between vendors (particularly independent contractors) you use versus employees. Peripheral functions, like payroll services and freight delivery, can be safely and easily outsourced to save money. Key operational functions should be brought in-house to be performed by employees. Every industry and situation is different and will change over time as the company grows. Technology offers greater efficiencies, so you should review the efficiency and effectiveness of your operations annually, if not more often.

26

Peer Accountability & Community Involvement

Developing a spirited corporate culture that reflects your values and goals requires much more than repeating those items to employees, vendors, and customers. Or simply providing direction, even though those are important. Similar to parenthood, your employees and other enterprise stakeholders will watch how you behave. This requires personal discipline on your part to actively and frequently pursue self-improvement.

Personal growth involves reading and networking with other businesspeople to keep abreast of developments in your industry, general business trends, and competitor announcements or actions in your community. Perhaps including self-improvement books or hiring a coach to help you with a skill you feel needs shoring up can enhance your effectiveness as a leader and innovator. As a Christian, the most important element of improving your leadership is regular Bible study.

Entrepreneurs are naturally independent-minded and highly self-confident, able to face the strong winds of adversity. They have extraordinary perseverance and are willing to try innovative ideas. This group of characteristics is referred to as **intrinsic motivation**—no need for peer approval or validation from others. These characteristics inherently seek leadership and responsibility to make things happen. Such an autonomous spirit is necessary to start and grow a business or nonprofit organization against all the negative expressions of doubt from others. Yet, the concept of personal accountability is a fundamental Christian principle, even though it goes against the independent-minded nature of entrepreneurs.

Accountability

Accountability for entrepreneurs involves not only market discipline imposed by competitors, vendors, and others. It should also reflect the three areas of intellectual development. Most people are familiar with **IQ (intelligence quotient)**, reflecting the knowledge and rational thinking skill level. There are two other types of intelligence. The first is referred to as **emotional intelligence (EQ)**. EQ refers to the ability to manage one's own emotions and the emotions of others. In a work environment, emotional intelligence involves perceiving control over your emotions to reflect appropriate positive, motivating behavior when helpful and refraining from displaying distress or anger when this could negatively affect those around you. It also involves recognizing other people's emotions and conveying empathy for them, plus identifying or relating to them effectively. Other EQ elements involve adapting to each environment or circumstance to help employees, customers, vendors, and other stakeholders arrive at mutually beneficial outcomes.

The second type of intelligence is **spiritual intelligence (SQ)**. As you may expect, this type of intelligence is grounded in firm values and beliefs expressed as vision, including the ability to effectively apply deeper meaning and purpose to thoughts and activities. For Christians, the basis of SQ would be the Bible. SQ involves self-awareness and utilizing a holistic approach.[28] SQ also includes developing the capacity to face and use adversity for good, and the ability to reframe situations into a larger context of meaning and purpose for yourself and others.

In addition to these personal leadership development efforts, you should ensure a balance of work, family relaxation time, worship, prayer, and community or charitable endeavors. The twin purposes for setting an example of balance among life's obligations and opportunities are for your personal renewal and effectiveness, plus modeling a supportive company culture that encourages employees to do likewise.

---

[28] Seeing the connectedness and sinful brokenness of actions, individuals, and circumstances.

Community

Informal community engagement could include hiring one or two welfare recipients and working with local churches to help those new hires build personal self-respect and confidence to overcome any troubling background problems holding them back. Employees can also be encouraged to participate in local informal and formal charitable activities in the community via both voluntary payroll deductions (which your company might partially match) and volunteer time (which you possibly could encourage by instituting a paid charity time off program). Community involvement might encompass some social responsibility programs, especially with Christian organizations. Alternately, environmental stewardship efforts are another area your company can engage in.

As your company grows, new opportunities for community engagement open up. For example, some Christian businesses contract corporate chaplain services to employees. Others form a charitable nonprofit corporation to channel their company's donations, while other entrepreneurs join boards of local charities. There are various ways to create connections to the local community and join with fellow Christian entrepreneurs to impact people in the marketplace with the Gospel. As Christians, the important point to keep in mind is we are called to engage the culture with God's message, not to stay disengaged or narrowly focused only on building profits and trying to stay non-controversial.

How can you keep on track with your personal goals and assure you have not drifted away from God's purpose for you and your business? Simply joining business associations for networking and prospecting purposes will not keep you accountable. As pointed out earlier, the highly independent nature of entrepreneurs, combined with a very limited number of people you can safely open your heart to, can make staying on course extremely difficult. Employees are not at risk for all expenditures and for generating revenue as you personally are. Neither they nor suppliers will suffer the full impact of mistaken decisions. The worst an employee can do is earn zero. Vendors will cut off credit to limit their losses.

In contrast, the entrepreneur can lose everything they own and be forced deep into debt if they are not careful and cautious. Likewise, customers are almost always unsympathetic to or uninterested in understanding daily business challenges. Even family members rarely understand the unique pressures and challenges entrepreneurs endure.

Other Christian entrepreneurs provide an opportunity to practice sharing ideas and challenges as well as be held accountable for our Christian walk in our businesses and our personal lives. Fellow Christian business owners who have no actual or potential conflict of interest from their lines of work can provide empathetic listening and provide feedback on Biblical applications for current issues you face. They can also give each other comradeship by studying what the Bible has to say on business-related topics, and by praying for one another.

A small group of trusted Christian entrepreneurs helps hold you accountable to ethical and charitable efforts as well as personal conduct, as you pledge correspondingly to do for them. Such a focused small group should not be used as a forum to solve business problems, although the group might study Biblical concepts for common situations, such as incurring debt, providing surety, transactional honesty standards, how to deal with bad or unproductive employee behavior, and other issues all business owners face.

At this point, you may be wondering how to assemble such a group. The easiest course of action would be to join an existing group in your area. There are two international Christian entrepreneur organizations offering such groups and regional and national conferences, Bible study materials specially designed for business owners, and other support.

These two groups are Fellowship of Companies for Christ International (website fcci.org now also called Christ@Work) and C12 Group (website www.c12group.com).

There are other smaller organizations for Christian entrepreneurs throughout America and abroad. Perhaps you feel more comfortable building your own group and developing all your own resource materials from scratch. The important takeaway from this chapter is to seek peer accountability regarding how effectively you utilize your business as a platform for ministry.

VI

Business Modeling

This final section looks at progressing from your initial idea into refining it, to writing a plan that guides you towards achieving your vision.

Chapter 27 fleshes out the entire idea so we can test whether it is marketable.

Chapter 28 reviews methods for connecting marketing, operations, leadership, innovation.

Chapter 29 covers how to transition "failure" successfully when necessary.

Chapter 30, 31, 32, and 33 explores both the useful aspects of planning as well as the drawbacks.

27

Unique Value Proposition

Your **Unique Value Proposition (UVP)** is an innovative idea you develop as an entrepreneur. It might be unique in terms of technology or for reaching a particular market niche or combining products, services, and price. Or perhaps based on some other perception you believe potential customers will see as valuable. It is vital to develop your UVP to test your business concept well and have the opportunity to grow into a successful company. We will walk through each of the four elements of a UVP in this chapter. Try sketching brief notes or keywords onto a page describing each component.

Value Proposition

The first part of the UVP is the **value proposition**, sometimes called the **offering**. What is the need you are trying to solve, and what product or service do you propose to provide as the optimum solution? Don't simply mention a commodity.

Describe the features of the product or key contributions of the service. What aspects of your offering do you hope will be most attractive to potential customers? What is of secondary importance to potential customers but may seem like nice add-ons as long as the primary need is met? What features are standard among competitors or taken for granted, and therefore cannot motivate potential customers to buy but must be included to have a workable product or comprehensive service? How might these essential but unappreciated factors be produced quicker, lower-cost, or in some other more efficient manner? How can they be fully integrated with attractive features to enhance the products potential customers are most interested in purchasing?

Customer

Second, who is your **customer**? A complete answer to that question would require a description of the typical type of person you hope will buy what you will be offering. What income range can afford your products and services? What are their interests? Which organizations do they belong to which you can target your marketing towards? How many potential buyers live or work within the target market range? Can you share your message with them in a language that is appealing and in an affordable yet effective set of marketing channels? What are the niches or sub-segments of potential customer groups with differing needs, uses, and desires for your product or service offering?

People

Third, what **people** do you need to begin and build the business? This element involves knowing what technical, marketing, operational, executive, and other expertise (both training and experience) are required to meet customer demands. The background should not be solely generic industry or professional expertise; for best results, the experience should be directly related to the mix of other components you intend to build.

Technology

Finally, describe the **technology** required to produce your offering. That does not mean it must be high-tech-related, although it might be. All businesses require some technology to operate, from low-tech forklift or truck to higher-tech software that requires specialized training. How will you finance any heavy technology purchases needed to start and grow your business? What expertise must you either hire or contract for to repair and maintain the equipment? Are there any extended lead times to bringing technology online, such as filing for a patent, obtaining a government permit or approval to market, or any other hurdles that mandate time, money, and regulatory approvals before offering to the public? Does your core technology or science have any distinctly differentiated aspects from competitors?

Unique Advantages

After comparing competitors' offerings, you should attempt to develop a unique advantage in each of these four critical areas. Each advantage by itself need not be huge, but the combination should be significant enough to attract the attention of a large group of prospective customers. While other UVP charts usually include three circles, we will include four. Draw four circles representing the four components of your UVP—offering, customers, staffing (or contractors), and technology. Inside the circles, write both the bland essentials and the unique advantages. The intersection of these four circles, where you provide the most alluring offering to your target market, is your value proposition to potential customers. Compare it and test it with marketing surveys to determine if it is unique enough to draw a significant amount of prospects away from their current suppliers.

Unique Value Proposition: Four Data Points

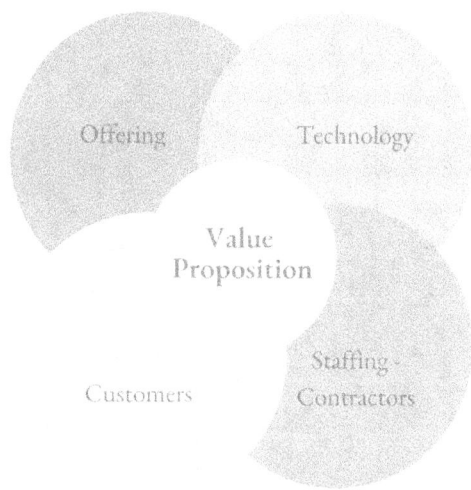

Another way to measure whether your UVP is truly feasible as a business model would be to informally develop (and then continually modify as you gain market knowledge) the following type of graph:

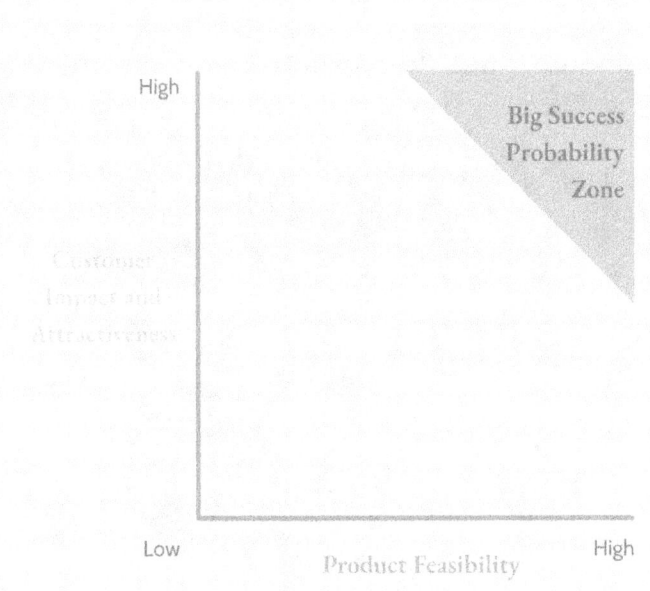

The triangle on the graph represents the intersection of high demand and high feasibility to produce goods and services that meet that demand. Suppose you can produce products and services with at least a sustainable profit margin that is in high demand by consumers. In that case, you will significantly increase your probability of building a successful company. The lower either factor is, the less likely you are to succeed. A low factor indicates a need to revise your idea.

Revising Your Plans

Of course, rarely do plans go as planned. Many entrepreneurs find they must undergo several revisions and sometimes morph into totally new business models before arriving at a refined idea with a high probability of success. Before committing large amounts of capital towards building infrastructure, consider ways to test your idea on a small scale. Track key variables on a spreadsheet to test how rapidly you can ramp up sales. Study how some competitors price and operate their businesses successfully and how others set up their business models but failed. Then write up your hypothesis on how you intend to provide a profitable product or service and why potential customers will be excited to purchase it.

Track the revenue, gross profit margin, operational time to produce or provide your offering, cash flow,[29] and similar key tests to prove your UVP truly has a realistic potential to become a sustainable, profitable business model. Study the trends over weeks and months, setting a deadline for evaluating progress (or lack thereof) at the end of that period, whether three months, six months, or some other period. One of the key reasons to determine quickly whether your idea is sustainable relates to the burn rate. The definition of the burn rate is the investment capital you start with divided by the new company's average monthly cash outlays (or projected expenditures). That tells you how many months your startup company can survive before you are starved for cash and crash if sales do not grow substantially before then. The more initial

---

[29] Including an estimated timeline for the burn rate.

overhead you build, the faster your burn rate.

Testing your UVP involves conducting some marketing studies, as discussed in an earlier chapter, then beginning to sell on a small scale and making adjustments as required. Academic studies and interviews with entrepreneurs found most changes, even when leading to an entirely new business model or major revisions of the original idea, were implemented incrementally through continuous triple learning loop feedback, which involves a series of minor individual changes. The other aspect of refining your UVP that researchers uncovered is that most UVP adjustments result from spontaneous new insights (mostly from customers) regarding additional opportunities rather than recognition about areas of your UVP that are failing or falling short.

An Example

Let's illustrate how one entrepreneur developed and refined his UVP. This particular entrepreneur—we can call him Fred—is a pediatrician who thought he could serve his child patients better and faster by providing a mobile injections clinic to provide allergy, immunization and various vaccination, and other shots. To test this idea, he produced a brochure provided to every parent and asked if this would save them time if he brought the clinic to them rather than waiting in his office for an appointment. After sufficient feedback indicating this idea could attract both existing and new patients, we developed a spreadsheet for what it would cost to create and operate such a mobile clinic versus what amount and types of revenue sources we could obtain.

We also considered lost revenue from closing his office for a day versus what the mobile clinic might generate to arrive at a minimum number of shots provided to make this project profitable and sustainable. It took nearly six months of marketing among existing patients and having staff pass out brochures outside schools before a sufficient number of people responded positively to make this unique idea appear possible. Up to this point, the investment was only a few hundred dollars for printing costs plus a small portion of one employee's time and wages.

The next test stage involved a much larger increase in cost. Fred rented a van on a short-term lease and strapped racks inside the van to hold containers of various vaccinations and added a battery to power a cooling unit. He rescheduled patients to clear one day every two weeks for testing this idea. We also offered a referral discount waiving the standard visit copay if patients also brought their friends to the mobile clinic. Fred's initial target market was Medicaid recipients, so he focused on lower-income subsidized housing projects as initial locations to park the van.

Responses from parents lead to several modifications in the original UVP. Dave contacted the local public school system and found there was some interest in offering standard required shots, such as seasonal flu shots, to staff and participating students and their parents. However, the revenue generated was sporadic and gross profit was not sufficient to justify a regular route. However, this "failure" generated two new changes to the UVP. Some local businesses were willing to sponsor flu shots to keep employees healthy and working. The local government health service was also interested in pursuing a grant to contract with Fred for offering standard inoculations to recipients of government programs and their own employees.

Fred also realized that as his innovative new service gained additional publicity and referrals, he could lower per-patient costs. Now he could purchase the van instead of having to lease and train a nurse to provide the shots. He could also hire a marketing person to make contacts with other larger employers and government agencies in surrounding areas. The mobile clinic could service groups in target markets within a 100-mile radius. By the time Fred was ready to hire the marketing person and purchase the van, he had proven the modified UVP as a very successful idea that was ready from which to build out a business.

28

Core Competency Design

Your Unique Value Proposition (UVP) described in the previous chapter is the seed or kernel from which your company will grow. Think about the key areas which every business or nonprofit must develop:

- Marketing & Sales
- Operations / Production
- Human Resources
- Financial / Accounting
- Leadership

Some or all portions of the first four areas can be initially outsourced to partner organizations. In contrast, the final area—leadership—must remain with you. Eventually, this will expand to include a management team you develop as the company grows. While outsourcing often costs more per unit of product or service sold, it also provides flexibility. It also conserves initial capital until the new firm can overcome initial startup losses to extinguish the burn rate by achieving a sustainable level of sales. As sales increase, plan on gradually bringing some of these functions in-house. Productions and basic operational activities are most often the first areas to transition into internally produced activity. Next is usually the marketing and sales function.

Laying the Foundation

Plan on conducting marketing and production tests at regular intervals. A good metric is at least a couple of times per year to determine what aspects should be changed to improve market acceptance and internalize these and other functions. Set up measurement goals in advance for each activity cycle within the company and sales benchmarks. Be cautious: Setting up measurement tools and goals afterward all too often leads to leaders fooling themselves into thinking the company is progressing sufficiently.

Testing the market demand without risking much startup capital is the lowest risk approach. Offer discounts for initial customers as test cases, ramp up several production levels while stress testing system design at each step. Startup companies may be less profitable initially or even generate early losses. Be aware that losses are very common during the first year. The faster the growth goal, the more likely the losses will be larger and last several years longer than a smaller, slower growth corporation might experience. Also, aggressive growth goals may require you to modify your UVP or pivot to respond to other aspects of company operations and consumer demands.

A new company must grow from an embryonic core UVP into a fully operational business model in the startup and incubator stages. However, the model at this early degree of development is akin to infant development, including a significant amount of outsourcing and direct leadership "hands-on" participation in production and sales.

Successful startup companies build the core and scale cautiously, even when they grow rapidly. Thriving startups tend to have several common characteristics:

Start with the best-fit people. Spend the extra time to find a few great hires—or founders before you hire any employees. Hire people who are:

- Hardworking
- Self-motivated
- Passionate about your company goals and vision
- Skillful and experienced in their area
- Who understand what needs to happen to accomplish tasks without much supervision

When in doubt, outsource to a contractor, until you find the right employee.

You thoroughly understand your model. You have carefully studied the market niche and know what they want, where to find those potential customers, what sustainable profit margin they will support for the price and production expense you can operate at. You have a plan calculating the burn rate plus initial capital to support the company until it can achieve break-even. Better yet, you can effectively convey your understanding to employees.

Staying lean; avoiding temptation. Keep costs and asset expenditures low, allocating money towards creating more money, even as revenues grow. That includes not hiring until the workload becomes tough to complete, frequently testing product feature acceptance in the market before expanding production, conserving cash whenever possible, and responding quickly to changes in opportunities or threats.

Streamline whenever possible. Automate or at least outsource to vendors the most labor-intensive processes and activities. Concentrate on what customers perceive as the highest value, such as customer service, warranty work guarantees, or other key competitive benefits. If you are manufacturing products, consider outsourcing component fabrication, and bring just the final assembly and quality control check on as an internal function.

Promote guerrilla marketing efforts aggressively. Referrals usually take at least a couple of years to come in at any appreciable rate. Maximize exposure for your products and your company very early. Pour as much time and money into pushing increasing marketing. Marketing efforts are the booster rocket fuel that will send your company into a sustainable orbit, preventing a crash and burn situation from anemic revenue growth.

Keep your values and vision fresh. Review the business plan, compare actual performance against milestone goals, and take regular vacations with family to refresh your spirit and renew your perspective.

Conduct regular reviews of business process cycles. It is easy to miss the sight of the forest because you gradually let new trees grow to block your view. Constantly question how each activity might be done faster, more efficiently, in a greater customer-pleasing manner, or at a lower cost.

An Example

Let's consider an actual case history to illustrate core competency design. An engineer entrepreneur, Susan, lives in a rural county that is noted for high pork production. However, larger farmers were warned (and a few cited for significant fines) by the state and federal environmental protection agencies for the groundwater pollution the hogs were causing. Susan designed a patented methane generator that needed little oil and methane to transform the methane into a modest amount of electricity. She then attempted to sell the $250,000 generators to large hog farmers and made only a few sales due to the high price.

Fortunately, Susan subcontracted to produce most of the parts while she assembled the first few units. After six months of frustratingly poor response, Susan modified her UVP and core approach. Originally she sold units on the basis that her company's generator could partially offset the environmental fines by generating enough electricity to power the entire farm operations. Her newly modified idea helps eliminate government environmental fines and threats of shutdowns.

To accomplish this revised goal, Susan initially contracted with a trucking company to pick up hog waste from farms and carry it to a rented site. The site contained enclosed compost bins which "cooked" the hog waste, leaching heated water into an open area for further boiling to cleanse all toxins from the water. The vents in the compost area fed directly into a larger model of the methane generator, which outputs electricity. Taking advantage of a state renewable energy law, Susan contracted with the local power company to sell all the excess electricity her company did not use for the ovens. This generated a rapidly growing revenue stream. Susan also invited government environmental inspectors to tour her small facility and discuss the improved land and water cleanup on hog farms that her UVP was accomplishing. A letter from a state environment official affirming the benefits and suggesting participation in her program would eliminate fines as high as $25,000 annually, gave Susan a selling tool to sign up farmers for a $1,500 per month fee to haul their hog waste to the company's processing center.

As more farmers signed up, hauling and electricity reselling revenue streams were boosted. Susan then invested more money into producing marketing materials for other farmers and towards becoming involved in the area hog farmers association. Other portions of the increased revenue went towards building more and larger methane generators and bigger recycling bins. In addition, Susan used some of the electricity to power a superheating unit she designed for the compost bins, which in turn increased the electricity sold into the power grid and simultaneously increased the volume of hog waste that could be processed monthly.

Her initial first, then second, employees were excited about cleaning up their county, but they were stressed from the long work hours. By then, cash flow had increased enough over the first 18 months of operations that Susan could gradually hire more full-time employees while using temporary labor services to service surges in production when more than one or two larger farms signed up.

At approximately the three-year mark, the company was doing well. Susan approached the county commissioners to suggest they approve an economic development loan or bond to extend the county sewer system to her property and some of the larger farms. Susan's company would then repay the government loan, costing county taxpayers nothing, while partially solving the environmental problem. This enhancement allowed Susan's company to begin eliminating the trucking service expenses. Now the county sewer system was bringing methane-generating waste from farms directly to her composting bins, which were continually expanded. She also "borrowed" the county government's lower municipal bond interest rate, saving money and building larger infrastructure expansion than a private bank would be willing to finance for her company.

Currently, the company is gradually assisting the county government to extend the county sewer system throughout the entire county. This will eliminate the farmer fee income from hauling away hog waste. However, the huge increase in methane-generated electricity sales, combined with gradually eliminating all trucking costs, and avoiding any sewer/transport system maintenance costs (which are borne by the county government) have more than offset the lost revenue stream.

While electricity is the primary revenue stream, the company has discovered two additional revenue streams, and a potential third new one. Superheating the hog waste to extract methane gas also vaporizes and cleanses the liquid into pure water vapor. This is then collected and cooled back into a liquid again. The water can be sold in barrels or bottles for a modest profit after paying for packaging, hiring staff (including a quality control biologist), and some additional marketing costs. After burning off the water and methane gas, the remaining solid from the original hog waste is a granular substance that can be sold as fertilizer through home improvement and hardware stores. The company is just beginning to explore another possible revenue stream—consulting fees from farmers to show them how to clean up hog waste pens and fields quicker, allowing them to increase hog production. That also boosts sales of clean water and fertilizer to assist in maintaining the health of their hog herds and land.

Note that Susan's original idea was to turn environmental

costs into a revenue stream for farmers. The company built only a few smaller units based on this idea before modifying the concept. Only after finding the optimum approach did the company ramp up its operations.

Over the entire period described in this case study, which was six years, the company did not commit large sums of money or dilute ownership by seeking investors; instead, it cautiously and gradually grew, adding major partners such as the county government sewer system, but only after proving the sustainability of the UVP. In the meantime, the company's office staff operated for several years out of a small old strip mall office until cash flow increased substantially. Then it applied for a rural development low-interest loan to purchase the land and place a mobile trailer on the plant property beside the compost bins, generators, and purification containers to serve as company headquarters for Susan, her bookkeeper, and her marketing manager.

This is a fantastic example of how to pivot nimbly when developing core operations in order to generate a fully sustainable company out of an original Unique Value Proposition.

29

"Failure" and Refining

How do you define failure as an entrepreneur? Entrepreneurs define failure as giving up. Nothing short of that definition can properly be considered a failure.

The classic example of this thinking is Thomas Edison's comment about inventing the light bulb. When others falsely claimed he had failed, he calmly replied that he had succeeded in finding 10,000 ways the light bulb could not be created, making him closer than ever to succeed. That stubborn confidence did eventually lead Edison to invent not only the incandescent light, but also an entire industry. That same attitude also helped him invent other new industries, such as the motion picture business.

Refinement of the business is separate from failure. And refinement is necessary in order for the business to grow. Think of it like pruning a tree: cutting away the dead or dying branches allows the rest of the plant to live, succeed, and grow. It is the same thing with entrepreneurship: Be prepared to prune.

Rethinking Your Ideas

Very few entrepreneurs succeed without modifying their original ideas, as illustrated in Susan's case described in the previous chapter. The key is to not commit too much funding and time towards an idea until it is proven to generate a sustainable profit sufficient to support the entrepreneur plus additional growth. Sometimes innovation comes from a new insight, while other times change is forced by market forces. Consider the following two examples from the banking industry for market circumstances forcing entrepreneurs to rethink their ideas:

Firstly, today's JPMorgan Chase Bank, NA is the result of approximately 1,200 different financial institutional mergers and acquisitions. The very first company, founded by former United States Vice President Aaron Burr in 1799, was The Manhattan Company. The New York legislature approved the Manhattan Company charter to bring clean water to the Town of New York[30] through the wild Manhattan forests from the Bronx River.

The mounting cost soon became too demanding to construct and maintain the pipeline. Therefore, the company petitioned the legislature to modify the corporate charter to issue bonds and engage in financing activities. The company eventually

---

[30] Now the lower Manhattan Borough for the City of New York.

developed limited water company services, but the financial sector's potential quickly overshadowed the much lower profit potential from water sales. It did not take many years for the company to wholeheartedly embrace the banking business, selling off the water company, which the city eventually purchased.

Secondly, consider the radical change in direction made by the Wells Fargo & Co. partnership. Originally, the partnership was formed in 1852 by Henry Wells and William Fargo. The partners contracted with stagecoach companies to offer secured transport services to the general public, and store gold and other valuables for customers. As the business grew, the partners joined with other stagecoach companies to form the famous Butterfield Line, later operating the brief yet highly acclaimed Pony Express at the beginning of the Civil War.[31] Eventually, they expanded the revenue base enough to purchase many of their stagecoaches and horses to become one of the larger stagecoach transport companies in North America.

However, completing the first transcontinental railroad crushed the main stagecoach service, but the company continued to serve mining outposts and rural towns throughout the West where no railroad traveled. Despite the railroad competition, the company's business continued to grow into the largest stagecoach and transport service in America, serving some estimated 6,000 locations. Alongside

---

[31] While famous, this particular iteration of the business only lasted 18 months.

this service was the company's reputation for strongly safeguarding customer assets, especially gold and money. Wells Fargo offices gradually offered to increase banking services. The final death knell for the transportation company's main operations was World War I, when the government expropriated or forced out of business all the remaining company transportation services in 1918. From that traumatic event, the company, having reorganized itself as a corporation, applied for a bank charter and continued offering banking services through its many offices in states throughout the nation.

Although these two "banking" company examples have very different reasons for transitioning into the banking industry and from widely contrasting conditions, both firms were able to recognize new paradigms. Alexander Graham Bell presents a sharp departure due to his inability to recognize a paradigm shift. Bell invented the telephone in 1876 and co-founded the company eventually known as American Telephone and Telegraph Company (AT&T) the next year.

He also patented inventions in other fields such as hydrofoils, aeronautics, optics, and most notably, hearing aids. Sadly, Bell failed to recognize the incredible value of the telephone. As a result, he eventually lost control of the company he co-founded and never received the huge financial benefit from his major technological breakthrough. In a sense, although Bell was a very successful inventor and teacher, he failed as an entrepreneur. He gave up on the telephone, which he considered a distraction from the hearing aid work he felt would become more valuable. Remember, giving up constitutes a failure for an entrepreneur—don't repeat Bell's miscalculation!

There are many other examples of refining one's original idea and unique value proposition. Sometimes improvements cause a major change in direction. Consider the example of the Tappan brothers transitioning from the silk importer business into developing the credit reporting industry. Their publications would grow to include such prestigious publications as The Wall Street Journal, New York Journal of Commerce, Dow Jones & Co., Dunn & Bradstreet, and others. For other entrepreneurs, minor modifications combined with stubborn tenacity lead to success, as it did for William Colgate. His multiple "failed" general goods stores eventually brought him great wealth and a lasting legacy in a worldwide company (Colgate-Palmolive) that is still in operation over two centuries later. Furthermore, his Christian charitable legacy extends to the American Bible Society and Colgate University.

Downsizing, losing a business, or declaring bankruptcy is not a failure. Failure is quitting. The true entrepreneurial test is knowing when to adamantly persist versus when to pivot in the face of market pressures.

How to Pivot

Pivots are required when actual results differ significantly from projections in the business model. To determine this in a timely manner, an entrepreneur must first develop monthly financial projections and non-financial marketing benchmarks,[32] so you have assumptions to compare your actual data against, rather than flying blind. Then set timelines for analyzing results.

For example, an Internet product platform could set review points at six months, nine months, fifteen months, and two years. At each point, the entire company team should compare actual results against plan projections. Early adopter prospects and customers may create a temporary surge with their enthusiasm for trying new things. But the bulk of customers for nearly every firm are the mainstream "lump" in the old bell curve.

The bell curve is a key indicator, as the average consumer is less adventurous and simply wants a product or service that offers most of the main features they want along with easy usage for a modest or average price. If those mainstream prospects do not sign up in increasing numbers after the brief initial surge of early adopters, that is a clear signal the business model must be modified.

Frequent reviews of customer feedback and customer marketing pipeline metrics will allow the company time to pivot before the burn rate consumes all the initial capital. Downturns in prospect inquiry and signups and continued low conversions into paying customers point to an uninspiring business model that will fail unless modified. Conversely,

---

[32] Such metrics could include the number of prospects signing up for free, the conversion volume from free to paying customers, etc.

a slower but steady conversion rate into paying customers probably indicates you should persevere and cut costs as much as possible. Then your company can survive a longer financial runway until achieving liftoff with positive, sustainable cash flow.

There is definitely a subjective element to the entrepreneurial judgment call on when to swivel versus persisting. Yet only a minority of such decisions are difficult to call. Customer and prospect feedback and the statistical data often provide clear guidance on when an adjustment in the product, marketing approach, pricing, or some other element of the business plan should occur. The key to successfully leveraging your metrics are frequent honest comparisons between actual performance versus your original assumptions and hopes as reflected in the business plan—and the critical element of learning from your mistakes while being humble enough to institute swift correction.

Why Startups Fail — Or Succeed

Many startup businesses fail because an entrepreneur insists they know better what the customers will pay for than the customers themselves. However, such vain hopes or personal stubbornness harm the business and increase the likelihood that the business model will buckle, as every business can cover its expenses and pay a profit to the founder only from revenue derived from customers. This is true even for non-profit organizations where a group receiving services differs from those supplying the revenue in the form of donations or grants. If your revenue stream (the people with the money) is not convinced your product or service is worthwhile enough to hand over some of their cash, your model will fail. It doesn't matter how "cool" you think it is. The harsh truth is this: If you don't succeed, nobody cares about the model you employed to launch the business.

Many successful startup companies make a series of business model alterations before finding an ideal approach that generates substantial revenue streams. Admittedly, it is emotionally difficult to give up on one's vision and instead let customers steer the final shape of your carefully designed and nurtured corporate baby. But it must be done if you want the business to succeed.

This is backed up by countless examples and research studies conducted by the United States Small Business Administration. They confirm that multiple modifications of a business over time will be necessary. Some changes will be small pivots, a few will be large modifications. Either way, pivots are inevitable in most startup companies for your tender startup to grow into a mature, strong company. It's a natural process that, like pruning a tree, can result in substantial growth.

Be intentional in this process. The more objective the statistical analysis of variances from your original projects are, the easier it will be to overcome the natural emotional tension that causes so many new entrepreneurs to sink with their original vision rather than soar with modifications provided by customers. Be prepared to step back, and stop clinging to an idea simply for the sake of the idea itself. Remember, pivoting based on customer feedback does not void the most important point—the business model is still your vision and idea. Rather, it allows your business to flourish, positioning it for growth.

30

Uses for Plans & Budgets

Many entrepreneurs grumble about preparing a business plan. However, they are necessary. Investors and bankers typically require a business plan before considering whether to provide funding. Even if you are not seeking outside funding from others you may still obtain a substantial benefit from preparing a business plan for yourself. The two main advantages of a business plan are to prove to yourself and any funding sources you may solicit that you have thought through all aspects of the business model, including accounting for what might go wrong. And you have a reasonable possibility of achieving success by following the path laid out in the business plan. Without a business plan, you are flying blind. To quote an old small business proverb: If you don't develop a business roadmap, don't expect to arrive at your desired destination. In most cases, you increase your probability of success by preparing an initial business plan, and then using it as a benchmark to track progress, modifying as needed to pivot from the original model.

What exactly is a business plan? And what is the purpose of each section? A typical business plan includes the following sections:

- Executive Summary
- Mission
- Industry Description & Analysis
- Market Analysis
- Marketing & Sales Plan
- Management Team
- Operations Plan
- Financial Projections
- Risk Factors
- Exit Strategy (if you are seeking outside funding)

In addition, a Christian or marketplace ministry version of the business plan can expound on their Christian ethical principles in the following sections:

- Core Values
- Goals & Objectives
- Non-Financial Measurement Criteria

Let's examine the purpose of each section. The order below is the common sequence for nearly all business plans. I have inserted the Christian marketplace ministry sections into sections you would typically find in a report.

Executive Summary

An Executive Summary is exactly what it sounds like. This is a one, or possibly two-page, section. It's a compilation of the entire plan's approach. It is the last section you as the entrepreneur should write, but the very first—and often only—section a potential funding source will read.

So, make it pithy and attention-grabbing. It has to grab the reader's attention with an exciting investment opportunity and the impression of a thoroughly considered and realistically possible execution for the idea. If you lose them here, the rest of the report, however brilliantly executed, will only be glossed over. If the executive summary does not excite a potential investor immediately, they will throw the plan away without reading any of the details.

Venture Capital (VC) firms are swamped. Most report receiving an average of 100 to 200 business plans daily. If each plan is approximately 50 or so pages, multiply that number, and that's 1,000-2,000 pages of data to wade through each day! VC firm employees cannot possibly read all the plans, which is why they skim only the executive summary. This is a way to screen out reports. Most firms select only around one percent of the plans submitted to inspect further. Less than 10% of those (in other words only 1 out of the original batch of 1,000 submissions) attracts enough interest to merit detailed testing of the full plan's assumptions and projections.

The primary reason most investors and many banks, as well as the Small Business Administration, reject business plans is that they feel that the entrepreneur does not really understand what it will take to monetize the idea and build revenue. Both are necessary to sustain success.

Mission

The mission section explains briefly what marketplace needs you are trying to meet. In this section, you must not only describe your idea, but also give an overview of why you think potential customers will be interested in purchasing your solution, and why competitors are not meeting this need or missing a gap in coverage.

Core Values

For a Christian entrepreneur, it is not nearly enough to merely earn a profit. As representatives of Jesus, the Christian entrepreneur has a special obligation in this section. As they pursue business growth and the evangelism and discipleship opportunities that are a natural outgrowth of business relationships, core values are a chance to open the door to deeper conversations. It's a natural way to state the entrepreneur's goals as they use their business venture to fulfill the Great Commission. It's a way to demonstrate to people who may never enter a church, or hear the Gospel message, what the core principles of the Gospel are. In this manner, core values are a reflection of the Gospel.

We should also recognize that we do not truly own the company we start. The entrepreneur is a trustee for God. Thus, the entrepreneur should seek to provide a Return **on Investment** (**ROI**) in terms of spiritual results. How you choose to operate your company conveys a witness—good or bad—and either opens or shuts opportunities to share God's Word.

To provide greater intentional and consistent witness, you should describe the key values you want yourself, your advertising, employees, and other aspects of your business to convey. These can include general "good business practices" concepts such as honesty, customer guaranteed satisfaction, and similar values plus hallmarks of the Christian faith, such as community active charitable involvement, sacrificial giving of time and money, holistic care for employees, servant leadership, and other related values.[33]

The purpose of the core values section is to state clearly the organizational culture you intend to create and utilize this section as a reminder for yourself and your employees of which values should rule when addressing difficult business situations.

Goals & Objectives

The difference between goals and objectives is simple. **Goals** are long-term oriented, typically intended to require more

---

[33] For real-life examples of this in the businesses of Christian entrepreneurs who transformed society, you can read my book Transforming Entrepreneurs.

than a year—sometimes many years—to achieve. **Objectives** are short-term "sub-goals" that move the company along the path towards accomplishing the larger goals.

For every organization, including charities, there must be financial goals. An increasing number of companies also add both social responsibility goals and environmental goals. Christian companies often include spiritual goals. Together these four sets of goals are referred to by academics as **Quadruple Bottom Line Goals.**

Goals and objectives should be specific, measurable, have a set time frame, and be realistic or achievable. It is easiest to develop financial goals that meet these criteria, but others are often more difficult. **Social and environmental goals** can be harder to measure, which is why larger "socially conscientious" corporations and large charities tend to measure or quantify their "results" by good intentions or efforts expended, rather than reflecting results attained.

Spiritual goals are the most difficult to measure, particularly since we humans can convey God's message, but only the Holy Spirit can perform the actual work of conversion. Nonetheless, it is possible to plan out spiritual goals.

Industry Description & Analysis

This is the section where you describe the industry, countries' marketplace characteristics (if starting an international business), growth rates, industry or niche trends, segmentation, long-term prospects, and similar characteristics of the market environment you plan to enter. Here are some questions to consider:

- Who are the major players in your industry?
- What are the major issues the industry is currently facing?
- What are the key success factors most competitors pursue?
- Is government regulation a problem facing this industry?

Industry analysis should be more than generic and superficial. Demonstrate you understand the nuances of profitably competing against more established players.

Market Analysis

Describe the target market size and trends, buyer behavior, competitor strengths and weaknesses, your best guess of competitors' sales volumes and trends, and other market survey data that conveys your deep understanding of what potential buyers will purchase, and at which price points.

Don't forget to include challenges from stronger competitors. Investors will not believe that you thought of the perfect solution that no competitor can beat! The main purpose of this section is for you to think through how you will cope with your competitors' strong points, and exploit their weak points, for meeting buyers' desires. This is in addition to documenting your research proving you understand what buyers are seeking.

Marketing & Sales Plan

Having described the industry environment and the competitive challenges in your chosen market, this section describes in sufficient detail your overall marketing strategy. How do you intend to position your products and services within the market, what you see as your strengths or advantages, and why your pricing is optimum in relation to what buyers are indicating that they will pay and what competitors currently charge?

This section should also explain your advertising and promotional strategy, product and related promotional mix, what distribution channels you intend to develop, a projected time frame and explanation for how you arrived at that time period, and of course your sales strategy. It is also helpful to include after-sale servicing plans, warranties, and other cross-selling efforts. This also ties in with your promotion of core values.

Management Team

Investors in any startup are not really infusing capital into a viable company at first. Rather, they are entrusting their cash to you, the entrepreneur, and your management team. It is your personal reputation at stake as well as your business reputation moving forward. The management team section needs to prove that you have all the leadership needs covered, whether by you, a partner or officer you bring in, outsourced to a vendor, or perhaps partially supplied by an advisory board. In this section of the plan, you outline personnel needs and illustrate your expertise in the industry and build confidence that you are likely to achieve the business plan milestones before invested money runs out.

Operations Plan

Whether producing or buying products or services, you must demonstrate that you can deliver in a timely manner on what you sold, and do so with sufficient quality and cost controls to generate a profit. You need not mention every minor step in your planned operations, but it is definitely important to provide enough depth to give the business plan reader a confident feeling that you can follow through with what you promise.

Financial Projections

All the previous sections are summarized in a numerical fashion in the financial projections. These commonly include the three main financial statements:

- Balance Sheet
- Profit or Loss Statement
- Cash Flow Statement

Each one of the above statements is projected month by month for the first 12 months. This is followed by annual projections for the next two years.

Since nearly all startups lose money during the first year, the **Cash Flow Statement** is the most critical projection to prove you are investing or requesting sufficient cash to cover the expected burn rate. Within the Profit or Loss Statement, you should build in a "miscellaneous expense" item for the unexpected, and take a conservative approach to delayed receipts. As we discussed earlier, late payments create financial stress, especially in small to medium-sized businesses, so it is best to mitigate this risk as much as you are able.

In my opinion, the most important element to financial statement projections, usually referred to as **Pro Forma Projections**, is the footnotes. If investors have enough interest to look at the financial statements they will want to know your reasoning for each and every number on every statement. That is the purpose of the footnotes, especially in regard to sales and receipt of cash. It is very easy for anyone to project spending lots of money, but very difficult to generate cash coming in. Therefore spend extra time detailing in the footnotes your reasoning for the sales volume and timing.

Some business plans will also provide a **Sources and Uses Statement**, which is simply a summary of what the initially invested funds will be used for. Note that the Pro Forma statements will include all this data anyway.

Non-Financial Measurement Criteria

As we have already noted, measuring non-monetary results is probably the most difficult part of any Christian business plan. Specifically, non-financial measurement criteria refer to how you can measure progress towards achieving social, environmental, and spiritual company goals. In public corporations, these are typically referred to as Environmental, Social, and Governance (ESG) reports, and many companies chose to include them in order to measure their impact on society, as a form of supplement to their financial reporting.[34]

Still, academic researchers, company presidents, investors, charities' boards, and grant-making organizations have all fallen short of being able to produce satisfactory measurement criteria for any of these areas. However, there are several approaches that you can apply to at least develop a rough benchmark. How to measure these seemingly intangible goals? To start, try approximating your progress towards the goals described in the early section of your business plan. Because there are not yet any sets of widely accepted measurements for these ESG criteria, it is important to list the ones you intend to use when reporting progress towards these types of quadruple bottom line goals. We will look at

---

[34] Notably, ESG analysis has become an increasingly important part of the investment process. Investors are incorporating ESG data into the investment process to gain a fuller understanding of the companies in which they invest. Christians should capitalize on these efforts, particularly as they have a unique value proposition to offer, given their moral objections to certain business practices, and support of social causes (and vocal opposition to others).

specific examples of such measurements later in this chapter.

Risk Factors

No endeavor, no matter how well established, is without any risk. Both you and any investors should be aware of what risks might throw your plan off track.

Perhaps you have some ideas on how to partially mitigate some of these risks. If so, list your ideas in this section, or cite research indicating the likelihood of each type of risk occurring during the company's first few years.

To give you an idea of the typical company risks, look through the risks section the Securities and Exchange Commission requires publicly traded companies to include in their 10-K annual report filings. It is usually listed under Item 1a, "Risk Factors" in the report. You can find reports on companies in your industry by going to www.sec.gov/edgar.shtml and conducting a company filings search.

For nonprofit organizations, the main risks tend to be related to fundraising fraud, reputation damage, quality of volunteer staff, data breaches, big swings in donations or grants, and not complying with tax or grant requirements.

Exit Strategy

This final section applies only if you seek investor funding. After investors have established a comfort level with your idea, and are reassured that you know the market, how to provide the product or service offerings, what your expected cash flow is, and that you have assembled a team that can get the job done, understand the key risks you cannot control, and so forth, the investors will then turn their attention to how they can make a profit.

Rarely do startup companies list their stock on a public stock exchange. Therefore, you need to explain how the investors will get their cash back with a rough estimate of the expected profit or profit range. Typical exit strategies include a company buyback after three to six years with a valuation based on either an independent business valuation expert's opinion or some predetermined formula or multiple derived from the cumulative profit or cash flow. Another exit strategy is to sell the company to a larger corporation in the industry, thus cashing out both investors and entrepreneurs. Expect your exit strategy to be a starting point proposal for negotiations with the investor, but not anything concrete.

31

Risk, Finance, & Christian Values

In Pathways to Nonprofit Excellence,[35] Paul Light states *"There is no single pathway to excellence."* He finds little evidence of what works and why it works in the achievement of high-performing nonprofits. Yet just because measuring human impact is difficult does not mean the effort is unproductive.

With non-financial goals, we are attempting to report innovative disruption, asymmetric growth, and market solutions (in the case of social and environmental challenges) plus support for God-supplied human intervention (for spiritual goals) to human-generated problems.

---

[35] Pathways to Nonprofit Excellence, Brookings Institution Press, Washington, p.37 (2002)

Measuring Progress with Non-Financial Goals

Measuring progress towards non-financial goals can be challenging. Qualitative factors are generally not quantifiable by their very nature. Yet, tracking progress keeps you accountable for moving to your desired outcome. Phrased another way, if you fail to plan, you are planning to fail. Goals and systems for tracking goal progress create behaviors and reinforce habits. Adding small incentives and rewards to encourage steps towards non-financial goal completion will gradually build the organizational culture supporting non-financial goals.

What methods have researchers and entrepreneurs developed to track progress on social and environmental goals? Both qualitative and quantitative measurement methodologies are in current usage. For both types, it is important to isolate the variables that drive program results. All current tracking efforts are accounting-oriented and derive from two key research efforts:

1. The **Rockefeller Foundation** brought together a group of charity and philanthropic executives in 2007 to examine how to accurately measure which charities utilized donated funds more effectively.
2. **Social Return On Investment (SROI)** was developed by George R. Roberts and his Roberts Enterprise Development Foundation (now called REDF). It applied for-profit business analysis to the charitable-oriented sector.

Rockefeller Foundation

The Rockefeller Foundation grouped measurement tools into three categories:

- Rating systems (for screening potential projects)
- Assessment systems (for summarizing results)
- Management systems (for assuring reliable ongoing tracking efforts)

Most measurement instruments or systems are assessment systems, but a number of them also overlap into one of the other categories as well. Many of the systems developed are modifications of a few basic measurement models. Let's explore the most popular models, which are used by businesses, nonprofit organizations, and "investors."

Business entities

Remember the **B Corporation** idea from the chapter on choosing your business entity? **Balanced Scorecard** is another B-corporation type of rating. This system measures operational performance in four outcome areas: financial (as in community impact, not company profitability), customer, business process, and learning or growth towards more socially and environmentally sensitive efforts.

Metrics include:

- Social impact
- Constituents served
- Internal processes
- Learning and growth
- Financial benefits to the surrounding community
- A "lives touched" qualitative and quantitative description
- Program quality customized to local needs
- Building critical organizational capacity and competencies

These variables are assigned a numerical value in reference to a benchmark consisting of two groups—high-impact organizations in the same nation and high-performing nonprofit organizations. Over half of the Global 1,000 largest companies participate annually in the Balanced Scorecard reporting, along with an increasing number of nonprofits, the federal government, and many school districts.

Qualitative Measurements

Qualitative consulting measurements, which are inherently subjective, are designed to compare against benchmarks. More accurately, they are designed to compare "best in class" criteria for the particular industry or service sector the company or nonprofit is involved in. Examples of such measurement systems are **Charity Analysis Tool (CHAT)**, **Compass Investment Sustainability Assessment**, and **Dalberg Approach**. The obvious drawback is the "eye of the beholder" type reporting on the amount of progress towards achieving social and environmental goals. This problem is supposedly offset by paying certification or audit firms specializing in these types of analysis to conduct the measurements and prepare the reports.

Some measurement instruments are the "check the box" variety. They are popular because it makes them easy and straightforward to determine if the social and environmental targets are met, but they cannot indicate the quantity or percentage of how much or little the organization has met the minimum requirements. Examples of this approach are **Fair Trade Certification**, **LEED Certification** (for environmentally friendly building construction standards), and **Guidestar Common Results Catalog**.

Quantitative Systems

An increasingly popular type of measurement is **quantitative systems**. Some of these are easy to understand. For example, Movement Above the US $1 a Day Threshold tracks company or nonprofit effectiveness in helping individuals or families in their communities rise above this poverty income level. Another example is **Progress Out of Poverty Index (PPI)**, measuring the number of microfinance customers moving out of poverty, as defined by the poverty level of the country in which the organization operates. Likewise, **Real Indicators of Success in Employment (RISE)** is an internal tool for monitoring how many poor people an organization hires, and how fast they move out of poverty as a result.

Some tools are designed for use by specific industries, such as the **Social Value Metrics** system, which helps banks lending to agribusinesses report on progress. This system uses fifty data points towards making an environment healthier and farming more natural (non-chemical) while minimizing negative impacts to surrounding land.

Social Return On Investment (SROI)

Now for the second method. In 1997, the SROI concept was developed by REDF and George R. Roberts. Roberts was co-founder of KKR, a major global private equity investment firm. He sought to apply similar analysis from the for-profit business world to the charitable-oriented sector, rather than continuing to rely upon the traditional "feel good" or "good intentions" approach that provided no accountability from charities.

Returning to the second major influence on triple bottom line measurement tools, the **Social Return On Investment (SROI)** has rapidly become the most widely used approach to measuring return on "investments" in social and environmental efforts.

There are multiple variations of the SROI approach:

- SROI Analysis
- SROI Calculator
- SROI Framework
- SROI Lite

- SROI Toolkit

Additionally, there are systems based heavily upon SROI such as **Social Impact Assessment (SIA)** and **Trucost**.

SROI is based on the desire of donors or investors to obtain more social and environmental benefits for their investment. Increasingly, charities are seeking to fulfill their missions through self-sustaining revenue-generating sales rather than rely upon unstable donations. Simultaneously, businesses are adding social and environmental goals, blurring the distinction between nonprofit and business status.

Charity-minded investors are moving towards providing loans with below-market-rate interest rates rather than outright donations so charitable funds can be recycled and **Return on Investment (ROI)** for charitable efforts can be monitored. SROI developed out of a transition in donor mindset that moved from charitable good feelings or good intentions to some form of provable return to either the investor or people in the community to the desire to quantify those efforts in order to get to the cut and dry business of how much money provided what amount of benefit. In other words, the emphasis is for charities and "socially conscious" businesses to prove results. Investors want to drill down and see exactly where their investment went, and ideally quantify in precise detail the benefit provided to the community. What was the impact of a philanthropic investment? ROI is an attempt to provide greater oversight in order to assess this question, and hopefully, improve future results for both the philanthropist and the cause receiving the money. Sure, it still makes the investor feel good, but it's backed up by hard statistics and data points, alongside human stories of how the initiatives impacted them.

SROI requires two reports. The first is a **forecast report** which predicts how much social value will be created if the activities meet their intended outcomes. This includes establishing the scope and identity of key stakeholders and **mapping outcomes**. Other elements of the forecast document evidence of likely value derived from the proposed effort, **establishing impact**.

The forecast then attempts to quantify in monetary terms the SROI as the value of added community benefits from the prior step, minus any negatives. The final section of the forecast report explains report frequency, how the report will be utilized, and how the organization will embed the results in its operations so continued learning and growth towards the goals will continue.

The second SROI report is the **evaluative report**. This report assigns monetary values to the actual results. These results are compared to internal earlier reports or forecasts to quantify the volume of progress and dollar value of net benefits as a result of the investment. This report utilized seven principles in the report:

1. Involve stakeholders in defining what gets measured and how.
2. Understand what changes occurred and how they were created. (Isolate the variables driving program results.)

3. Value things that matter, using financial proxies to recognize values.
4. Only include what is material.
5. Do not over-claim. (Subtract results from other societal factors to arrive at what your organization actually caused.)
6. Be transparent by demonstrating the basis on which the analysis is claimed.
7. Verify the result through an independent auditor that your decisions in formulating the report and calculating the results are reasonable.

A very recent adjustment to SROI evaluative reports reflects some form of beta adjustment or risk adjustment. The concept derived directly from stock investing—**Capital Asset Pricing Model (CAPM)**—adjusts return for risk. Since there is no widely reported marketplace for charitable efforts as there is for stock market assets, the coefficient of risk for charitable investing should reflect the difficulty or barriers to serving a particular population.

For example, a private school operating in an affluent suburb would have a lower "at-risk" population of students than a school educating children growing up in either rural or urban poverty with rampant unemployment, drug problems, high crime, and parental indifference to education. Therefore the Beta or risk coefficient would be adjusted for the estimated additional difficulty in helping children in the second school's environment.

Thus, the same charitable investment would yield greater risk-adjusted results in the second example. The concept is sound, but the great difficulty, in this case, is assigning inherently subjective risk adjustment figures for each situation. This can be only partially offset through interviews with social workers, police, pastors, and other community support people to determine an average difficulty overcoming each barrier to success.

Some SROI reports, while continuing to be quantifiably oriented, include a **qualitative narrative** for donors who are seeking proof that their investments are achieving maximum efficiency and effectiveness. These include a numerical percentage called the **Efficacy Rate**. This rate expresses the percentage of participants in a social program self-reporting having experienced a positive outcome. A similar measurement is the **cost per outcome** compared to a benchmark average for similar programs, plus the volume of people reached and the time commitment received from each participant.

Another addition is called the **Impact Value Chain**. The idea is to quantify the relationship between leading indicators (activities and outputs) with outcomes and impact to determine the dollar value of the net benefit to the community. Impact reporting then compares that net benefit to the donation invested to arrive at effectiveness yield. This helps large donors and entrepreneurs decide which programs or charities are higher performing choices for donation.

Since the SROI is investor-oriented, some businesses and charities have added another qualitative section addressing internal improvements. This is based on the **McKinsey Frame-**

work for Capacity Building, consisting of seven dimensions likely to increase an organization's positive impact on its community:

1. Aspirations—mission, vision, overarching goals, and direction of the organization
2. Strategy—a coherent set of actions and programs to achieve the overarching goals
3. Organizational Skills—performance measurement abilities, planning, resource management, and external relationship building
4. Human Resources—capabilities, experiences, potential, leadership commitment to non-financial goals, management team, staff, and volunteers
5. Systems and Infrastructure—planning, decision-making process, knowledge management, administrative controls, and physical and technological assets supporting these facets
6. Organizational Structure—governance, organizational design, internal and external coordination between functions, and organizational cultural artifacts bolstering desired attitudes
7. Culture—shared values and practices, behavioral norms, and organizational orientation towards performance

Two organizations have attempted to develop comprehensive reporting of all these quantitative and qualitative variables into a single reporting system. The first is called **IRIS+ Catalog of Metrics**, which provides a generally accepted impact accounting system of the most widely used impact performance metrics in a single system. The six key questions this system organizes data into are:

1. What is the goal?
2. Who is affected? For example, stakeholder type, characteristics, and demographics, such as client, customer, distributor, environment, community segment, etc....
3. How much change is happening? In particular, scale or breadth & depth of change.
4. What is the contribution? By enterprise and investor each, including identifying strategies.
5. What is the impact risk? Not only financial risk but risks from the involvement of target stakeholders, external risks from political/economic/social instability, market saturation risks, the dropoff risk of losing participants you are trying to help, etc....
6. How is change happening? For example, change in the range of product/service offerings, client engagement in each aspect of services, client repayment capacity, and non-financial client support offered.

The second organization, which has become the largest reporting agency for social and environmental goal reporting, is **Global Impact Investing Network (GIIN)**. Their website is thegiin.org. This organization defines four core characteristics of **impact investing:**

1. Intentionality—improving impact of social, environmental, or both types of goals
2. Investment with return expectations—the minimum return of capital, or actual positive ROI
3. Range of return expectations and asset classes (from

below-market or concessionary to risk-adjusted market rate across asset classes (such as cash equivalents, fixed income, venture capital, private equity)
4. Impact measurement (investor commitment to measure and report social & environmental performance and progress, ensuring transparency & accountability)

What Really Matters

We have examined a detailed summary of current best practices on measuring social and environmental goals. Whatever we do, we should not misconstrue tracking of triple or quadruple bottom line goal progress as a mere accounting exercise. Above all, God calls us to be good stewards of the resources He provides to us, and to be accountable, as in the parable example of the three stewards. Remember the idea behind quadruple bottom line tracking is leadership—not accounting. Rather, it is an effort to track and encourage greater pace and scale of systemic change for positive outcomes. At the risk of being called a heretic by my fellow CPAs, I think Christian entrepreneurs should emphasize leadership improvements, particularly in organizational culture, rather than just creating another accounting reporting system.

32

Spiritual Goal Setting

This leads me to the final quadruple bottom line goal-setting—spiritual goals for your business or nonprofit organization. As of the time this book was first printed there is no published research on spiritual goal setting for a Christian business. Some Christian business owners do include such goals within their own private business plans, while many others approach such ideas on an *ad hoc* basis. How might a Christian entrepreneur develop spiritual goals and measure their progress?

First, when there is tension between any of the four sets of goals, spiritual goals should always have priority over the other three (financial, social, and environmental). Spiritual goals should encompass the other three sets: the most comprehensive and holistic and should be acknowledged as such in writing your business plan.

Also, keep in mind conversion and growth towards spiritual maturity is the exclusive work of the Holy Spirit alone. As it says in Ephesians 2:8-9,

> *For by grace you have been saved through faith. And this is not your own doing; it is the gift of God, not a result of works, so that no one may boast.*

We've already discussed measuring social and environmental goals. Many measurement systems recognize that we often cannot control or quantify results, but we can measure effort, which helps contribute towards encouraging more of the desired attitude and actions.

Transforming Goal Setting with the Great Commission

Since no researcher or entrepreneur has yet published any attempts at measuring spiritual goals, we are breaking new ground. Let us humbly begin with several ideas for discussion, using three Biblical reference points as our basis:

- Matthew 28:18-20
- Deuteronomy 6:8
- James 1:22-25

Matthew 28:18-20

> *And Jesus came and said to them, "All authority in heaven and on earth has been given to me. Go therefore and make disciples of all nations, baptizing them in the name of the Father and of the Son and of the Holy Spirit, teaching them to observe all that I have commanded you. And behold, I am with you always, to the end of the age."*

The verbs from the Great Commission in Matthew 28:18-20 are translated as "go" (πορεύομαι), "make" (μαθητεύω) and "teach" (διδάσκω).

The Greek word translated as "go" is defined in Strong's Concordance "to pursue or continue one's journey; depart from life; to follow one and become his adherent; to lead or order one's life."

The English word "make" involves a specific Greek New Testament meaning "to be a disciple of one and follow his precepts and instructions; to make a disciple as in to teach and instruct."

The final original New Testament Greek word simplified as "teach" covers the following deeper meaning "to hold discourse with others to instruct them; be a teacher; to impart instruction, instill doctrine into one; the thing taught or enjoined; to explain or expound a thing; to teach one something."

Together, these three Great Commission verbs provide instructions on how to carry out our commissioning ourselves while simultaneously instructing others about Jesus' calling for our earthly journey, sharing His good news with as many people as possible.

Deuteronomy 6:8-9

> *You shall bind them as a sign on your hand, and they shall be as frontlets between your eyes. You shall write them on the doorposts of your house and on your gates.*

This "sign" (הוֹא) is to remind the Israelites of what God did for them and a prompt to teach their children about God's great love for them. The "distinguishing mark; banner; remembrance; miraculous sign; omen; warning; token; ensign; standard; proof" as Strong's Concordance explains this word's Bible usage, was physically manifested on their doorposts, foreheads, and hands.

Perhaps these three particular locations God commanded represent work or resulting handiwork creating shelter (doorpost), our thoughts (foreheads), and actions (hands). The Bible does not explain why these three particular locations were chosen for signage, but they may parallel the Great Commission's verb usage.

James 1:22-25

> *But be doers of the word, and not hearers only, deceiving yourselves. For if anyone is a hearer of the word and not a doer, he is like a man who looks intently at his natural face in a mirror. For he looks at himself and goes away and at once forgets what he was like. But the one who looks into the perfect law, the law of liberty, and perseveres, being no hearer who forgets but a doer who acts, he will be blessed in his doing.*

Looking at James 1:22-25, which emphasizes displaying faith through works.[36] The phrase "effectual doer of the Word" stands out. The original phrase is " ἔργον ποιητής λόγος" which can also provide guidance in our search for how to measure progress towards spiritual goals.

Strong defined the Greek word translated as "effectual" encompassing "business and employment; an enterprise or undertaking; not only a tangible product or accomplishment by hand or mind but also an act, deed, thing done; emphasizing work or action as opposed to that which is less than work or passive."

The second word, translated as "doer," is defined in the original Greek as "a maker, producer, author, performer or one who obeys or fulfills the law; a poet."

---

[36] Part of the cost of discipleship, or growing towards greater spiritual maturity and consistency.

The final "word"[37] is expansively defined as "a thought expressed, implication, topic or subject of discourse; reasoning or motive; cause; communication; doctrine; preaching; collection of such ideas, decrees, or mandates; moral precepts given by God; declaration; act of discoursing a weighty thought." James appears to be telling us that God expects us to be engaged in the employment of actively sharing Biblical truths through word and action.

As noted earlier, only the Holy Spirit can perform the work of conversion. So, that is not something we can set as a spiritual goal. However, God has invited us to play a role in sharing Biblical truths. That does not mean pushing Bible passages on customers, employees, vendors, and other stakeholders. It does, however, connote the idea of setting reminders, in line with the examples we've noted from Deuteronomy and tracking intentional efforts to live according to the model Jesus provided for us. First and foremost this involves your own example and witness to employees, customers, vendors, and the community.

Abide by Biblical company standards, such as going the extra mile for customers, not taking advantage of buyer or seller power over vendors but allowing them sufficient profit margin to survive and thrive, training and encouraging employees, showing care and concern for employees' families, and dealing honestly with all stakeholders.

In addition, spiritual goals might include developing a vol-

---

[37] In the Greek, it is pronounced "logos."

untary lunchtime Bible study with employees (which is *not* illegal—contrary to popular myth), encouraging employees to share their faith or offer Christian literature if someone asks about it, engaging in local volunteer charity and church projects, and pursuing similar goals that can be measured alongside qualitative and sometimes quantitative standards. The measurement of these kinds of activities can foster the organizational and personal culture and attitudes that guide moral judgments for business transactions and can make you and your employees more aware of opportunities to explore God's Word with others.

Operational Cycles

One way to begin exploring possible spiritual goals could be to consider the various operational cycles within your business. At each step, consider, "Where could a Biblical view make a significant difference?" How could you encourage people to consider such differences? Through ethical standards that witness to vendors and employees in your supply chain? This could include low-key symbols, literature, or employee greetings to customers that convey a different business approach to sales and service, or spiritual-based actions in other aspects of your business.

Case Study

Consider the following simplified case study illustrating how quadruple bottom line goals might provide a synergistic benefit to everyone involved in the company.

Suppose you own an urban gym and employ trainers as well as a part-time counselor or psychologist. Your vision is to market your business as a holistic health center rather than just a physical workout location.

A set of simple quadruple bottom line goals for this type of business might be:

Financial

1. Grow the customer base by 10% for the coming year.
2. Cross-sell training and counseling services for target groups for people with relationship difficulties like divorce or family death recovery, child-rearing, and so forth; weight issues; physical limitations; motivational challenges; or substance abuse problems.
3. Expand exposure by 20% among corporate HR directors and insurance agents selling subsidized health care plans.
4. Advertise and attract 25% increase in Medicare and Medicaid that's free to consumers, government-subsidized

"silver sneakers,"[38] and fitness memberships fee income.

Social

1. Develop three additional counseling niche programs to meet the needs of target groups.
2. Survey participants quarterly for feedback on satisfaction and rate of progress, identified barriers, and other indications of program effectiveness.

Environmental

1. Transition at least 50% of product sales for lotions, vitamins, and other items into offerings from environmentally friendly vendors without increasing the cost of products or sales prices to maintain customer affordability.
2. Sponsor a monthly community street and alley cleanup for two hours near the gym, inviting at least ten nearby churches, businesses, and community groups to join with employees, who will be paid for the time worked.

Spiritual

---

[38] SilverSneakers is a fitness program designed for the 65+ crowd that provides access to gym memberships, weight training, aerobics, and group exercise classes. Many Medicare Advantage plans cover SilverSneakers.

1. Conduct semi-annual surveys of members participating in self-help counseling groups about awareness of physical training, group counseling sessions on emotional issues, and interest in deeper group or one-on-one support.
2. Develop seminar presentations to explain holistic offerings to at least 10 churches.
3. Interview neighborhood pastors to develop a list of referrals and church resources available for customers seeking additional support and fellowship.

As an entrepreneur, you will be the leader to develop each goal to fit your vision for your business model. You are also the leader to recognize the opportunities for conveying greater multiple bottom-line benefits to the community, as Jesus calls us to do.

What's Next

Owning a business is a highly unique, personal expression of your own creativity, drive, and vision. Jesus is Lord of all—including our work as expressions of the abilities and experiences He gave us. Christian businesses should be platforms for marketplace ministry to reach people who might avoid churches but still need to hear about and feel expressions of God's love.

As entrepreneurs, we are trustees for the real owner of our businesses—God—who is looking for a quadruple bottom line Return On Investment in our lives to share His love and express His help to fellow humans. I hope this book has given you insight and actionable tools for launching and growing your business.

This book has provided a framework assisting you in methodically developing either a business or charitable organization. Most importantly, it has shown you how successfully your business, its impact, and your faith can be integrated into your day-to-day entrepreneurial activities. At this point, you should feel equipped to begin transforming the way you do business.

In this book, we have discussed major topics of vital importance to the entrepreneur, including big ideas of **Creativity, Marketing, Operations, Accounting and Finances, Cross-Cultural Leadership, and Business Modeling**. Most importantly, however, we have discussed **Spiritual Goal Setting** and how those goals should be incorporated into your business model, operations, and strategy.

What should be your ultimate takeaway from this book? It is my hope that you, an aspiring *Christian* entrepreneur, are inspired with this book's practical ideas for integrating your faith into your business and the marketplace. May God bless your efforts to start or grow a Christian business or charity that is an effective platform for marketplace ministry.

Continue Learning

If you are looking for additional help or want to learn more about Christian Entrepreneurship, then you're the person Entrepreneur Leadership Institute was built for. Visit Entrepreneur Leadership Institute now at:

www.EntrepreneurLeadership.net

This small 501(c)(3) international charitable research organization conducts research on leadership issues in entrepreneurial organizations of all kinds, with an emphasis on Christian leadership efforts. We are developing various resources, including a blog, podcasts, webinars, and low-cost online self-paced courses to provide deeper exploration on each aspect of Christian entrepreneurship described throughout this book.

Have a course in mind that you're dying to take? If you have a course topic in mind which we haven't developed yet (or may be in the works!) please reach out and let us know by contacting us now at:

        seminars@EntrepreneurLeadership.net

We look forward to hearing from you!

Dr. Kenneth R. Lenz

About the Author

Dr. Kenneth Lenz has started many companies, non-profit organizations and is a co-founder of a municipal government. He is also a CPA who has started, led, and sold several accounting and consulting firms across the United States. His firms have focused on providing services to smaller and rapidly growing entrepreneurial firms in various parts of the United States and several other continents. In addition, he earned a Ph.D. in entrepreneurial leadership.

From this unique background, he has studied and been deeply involved with entrepreneurship from the perspective of a serial entrepreneur in a variety of industries, as an adviser to many small business owners, and as a government official writing laws that affected business owners, in the profit-oriented as well as social entrepreneurship (social and governmental) sectors of the economy.

Dr. Lenz has also taught online business, entrepreneurship, and leadership courses on the bachelors, masters, and doctoral levels for universities in America and Europe. From these many-faceted viewpoints on entrepreneurship, he has also been involved in the international marketplace ministry movement for more than 20 years as a Christian entrepreneur.

Currently, he is chairman and founder of the Entrepreneur Leadership Institute. This small international research institute conducts innovative research in entrepreneurial leadership and shares those findings with entrepreneurs worldwide to help them improve society, both temporally and eternally. He is also developing a division of the Entrepreneur Leadership Institute which will offer training for individuals desiring to start and grow new businesses that can also engage in sharing the Gospel in the marketplace.